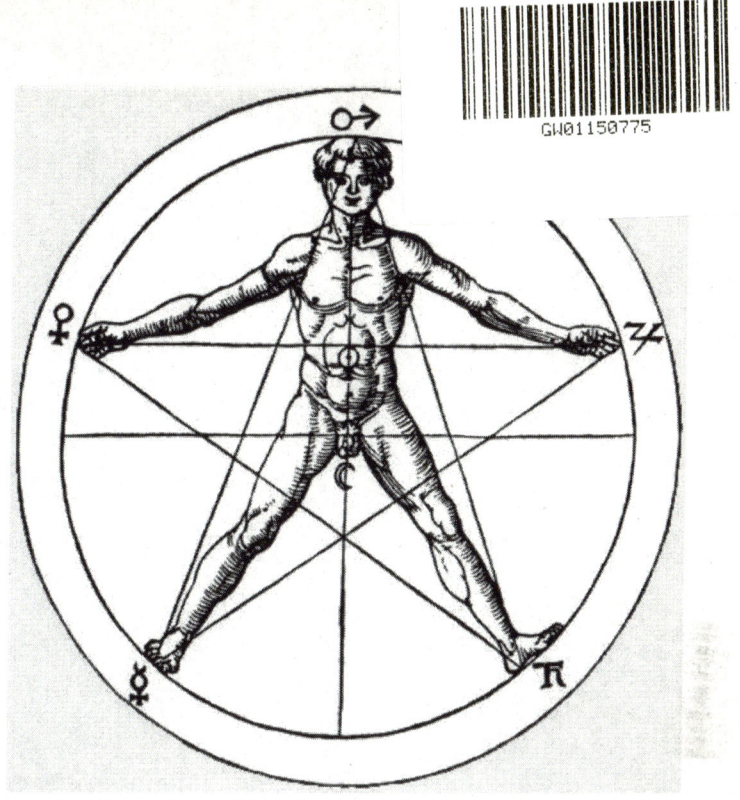

A Brief Guide to Personal and Psychic Development

TOTAL SENSORY PERCEPTION

alan

This First Edition 2013

ISBN : 978-1-291-44103-1

© Alan Jones

Everything I write in this book is a statement of my current understanding and offered as a set of ideas against which you, dear reader, can vent your spleen and challenge your thinking.

My aim is to provoke, to offer ideas and opinion and articulate presuppositions which, may sound like rules and laws, but are merely summaries of possibility.

© Alan Jones 2013

About this book.

The first part of this book deals with the definition of the word 'psychic' as well as a consideration of the presuppositions which underlie the decision to call someone or define yourself as psychic.

It explores ideas about intuition, consciousness and transpersonal experience.

The second part of this book outlines a seven week programme for 'psychic development' in the sense of developing 'total sensory perception'.

The general thesis of this work is that everyone is psychic and that when talking about psychic development we are, in point of fact, focusing on self-awareness and inter-personal communication skills. Where the individual chooses to take these ideas in terms of their own personal, spiritual philosophies (and hence the labels they choose to use) is a matter for each and every reader.

The third part of this book contains a number of exercises through which the reader can explorer, experiment and play with their increasing sensory awareness.

Where possible references have been cited and are fully indexed in the back of the book.

I hope you find your read interesting, challenging and ultimately rewarding.

Preamble

Words mean what we agree they mean!

The word 'psychic' has all kinds of connotations but for many implies a set of skills which some individuals possess, or claim to possess, that sets them aside from others.

It alludes to the ability to read minds, see clearly (the literal meaning of the word clairvoyant), to have mystical or extra-sensory experiences which help them see the world in very different ways.

The 'psychic' has been subjected to tests and experiments which seek to define their paranormal abilities...

The 'psychic' can be found inhabiting public venues at which 'spiritual guidance' and 'magical insight' is sought and offered...

The 'psychic' is presented by the media as someone who is special, different and who, by the virtue of their special talents, can be honoured or feared in equal measure.

The truth is, my friends, that such a restricted definition of the word 'psychic' has no place within a society which is seeking harmony, celebration of the human potential and personal development.

We are ALL psychic in the truest meaning of the word and in this short book I will argue that any human being who practices and develops 'total sensory perception' is, by definition exercising their psychic abilities.

For me a 'psychic' is an individual who is able to integrate sensory experience and intuition in such a way as to perceive the world in different, possibly unique, but certainly unlimited ways.

"Psychic" – A Considered Etymology

The word psychic probably derives from the Greek word 'psychikos' which refers to the human mind.

Psychikos in Greek can refer to something that is 'of the mind, mental'.

It seems that in classical Greek literature the term tended to be indicative of those 'better gifts and graces brought into the world by the gift of the Spirit'.

So on the one hand we have the idea that psychic refers to 'the mind' and on the other suggesting 'gifts and graces' given as spiritual gifts.

Christian writers and later Biblical scholars attempted to demote the word 'psychikos' and render it as a word referring only to the lower, more material aspects of the human condition, as opposed to the spiritual gifts bestowed through adherence to the teachings of Christ. Hence we find the idea that according to Scripture, the psychikos is one for whom the psyche is the highest motivation of life and action. (see Rom. 7:14; 8:1; Jude 19).

It was Paul who reminded the Ephesians of how they once behaved, "fulfilling the desires of the flesh and of the mind" (Eph. 2:3), he described them first as sarkikoi and then as psychikoi.

In this sense it is likely that *psychikos* was taken to infer natural or sensual whilst *sarkihos* suggested fleshly (of the flesh) or carnal. Hence Psychikos is one who is led only by the light of human reason and Sarkikos is one who is controlled by bodily desires.

Set against the background of the growth of Gnosticism, where knowledge was seen as being vital, this attack upon someone who is 'led by the light of human reason' can be seen as a call to the faithful to cease their questioning and simply accept the spiritual truths they are being taught.

Various Bible commentators have noted that:-

> *The question of how to translate psychikos is not easy to answer.*
>
> *"Soulish," which some have proposed, has the advantage of having the same relation to "soul" that psychikos does to psyche, but the word would certainly convey no meaning at all to ordinary English readers. Wycliffe translated psychikos as "beastly," which is equivalent to "animal" (animalis occurs in the Vulgate). The Rhemish Version has "sensual," and this was adopted by the Authorized Version in James 3:15 and Jude 19, instead of "fleshly," which appears in Cranmer's Version and in the Geneva Version.*
>
> *The other three times psychikos is used in the New Testament, it is translated as "natural." "Sensual" and "natural" are both unsatisfactory translations, but "sensual" is even more so now than at the time when our Authorized Version was made.*
>
> *The meanings of sensual and of sensuality have been modified considerably and now imply a deeper degradation than they formally did.* (Trench)

In Greek mythology, the maiden Psyche was the deification of the human soul. The word derivation of the Latin psȳchē is from the Greek psȳchḗ, literally meaning breath, derivative of psýchein, to breathe, blow, hence, live.

Psyche (Psykhe) : The Myth

Psykhe was once a mortal princess whose astounding beauty earned the ire of Aphrodite when men turned their worship from goddess to girl.

Aphrodite commanded Eros make Psykhe fall in love with the most hideous of men. Eros whose golden arrows make people fall in love accidentally pricked himself with one of his arrows and fell in love with Psyche himself.

He could not bear to do harm to her, so they got married and had a daughter named Hedone (called *Voluptas* in Roman mythology). Hedone is seen as the personification of lust.

Aphrodite said she would allow the marriage if Psyche could take a challenge and pass. Psyche was supposed to live with her husband without knowing who he was or what he looked like.

Psyche's sisters Orual and Thessela tricked her into believing that her husband might be a monster or that he might be cheating on her, so she lit a candle and looked at his face and found out he was Eros.

Eros stating that love cannot remain without trust and Psyche went searching for him. Her journey took her to Aphrodite.

Aphrodite said Psyche could get her husband back if she completed four tasks, the last one being to retrieve some beauty from Persephone (queen of the underworld) and bring it back to Aphrodite.

Psyche was curious and opened the box of beauty, only to find that it contained sleep instead.

Eros found Psyche lost in a deep sleep and asked Zeus to wake her up and grant her immortality. So Psyche was made immortal and a suitable wife for Eros.

Aphrodite now had no option but to give her blessing, Of course Psyche's immortality means she won't elicit the same attention from mortal men; she is no longer competition for her.

Psyche is depicted in ancient mosaics as a butterfly winged goddess in the company of her husband Eros. Sometimes a pair of Pyskhai are portrayed, the second perhaps being their daughter Hedone.

Gnosticism - Salvation through Knowledge

This definition, based on the etymology of the word (*gnosis* "knowledge", *gnostikos*, "good at knowing"), is correct as far as it goes, but it gives only one, though perhaps the predominant, characteristic of Gnostic systems of thought.

Whereas Judaism and Christianity, and almost all pagan systems, hold that the soul attains its proper end by obedience of mind and will to the Supreme Power, i.e. by faith and works, it is markedly peculiar to Gnosticism that it places the salvation of the soul merely in the possession of a intuitive knowledge of the mysteries of the universe and of magic formulae indicative of that knowledge.

Gnostics were "people who knew", and their knowledge at once constituted them a superior class of beings, whose present and future status was essentially different from that of those who, for whatever reason, did not know.

One of the things that many Gnostics 'knew' was that the world was created by an evil reflection of God, the Demiurge, which explains the existence of pain and suffering in the world, and that through gnosis the individual could attain salvation and possibly initiation into the light of truth.

The Psychic and The Spiritualist Movement

It was the French astronomer and spiritualist Camille Flammarion (1871) who is credited as having first used the word psychic, while it was later introduced to the English language by Edward William Cox in 1875

In both instances the use of the word became linked to the spiritualist movement and by 1885 a 'psychic' was one who was "characterized by having psychic gifts".

Spiritualism is a belief system which maintains that spirits of the dead residing in the spirit world have both the ability and the inclination to communicate with the living. Anyone may receive spirit messages, but formal communication sessions (séances) are held by "mediums", who can then provide information about the afterlife.

In many ways the gifts 'mediums' claimed were seen as being 'extra-sensory' in nature – i.e. communication using senses beyond the five we normally recognize hence psychic and hence 'sixth sense' (a term which became more popular in the 1950's)

Spiritualism developed and reached its peak growth in membership from the 1840s to the 1920s, especially in English-language countries and by 1897, it was said to have more than eight million followers in the United States and Europe.

The movement flourished for a half century without recognized texts or formal organization, attaining cohesion through periodicals, tours by trance lecturers, camp meetings, and the missionary activities of accomplished mediums.

Many prominent Spiritualists were women, and like most Spiritualists, supported causes such as the abolition of slavery and women's suffrage.

By the late 1880s the credibility of the informal movement had weakened due to accusations of fraud being perpetrated by mediums, and formal Spiritualist organizations began to appear.

Spiritualism emerged in a Christian environment and so has many features in common with Christianity, ranging from an essentially Christian moral system and Sunday services and the singing of hymns.

There are, however, some significant differences.

Spiritualists generally do not believe that the works or faith of a mortal during a brief lifetime can serve as a basis for assigning a soul to an eternity of Heaven or Hell; they view the afterlife as containing hierarchical "spheres", through which each spirit can progress.

Frequently a Spiritualists primary source from which they derive knowledge of God and the afterlife is their personal contact with spirits and spirit guides.

Most importantly, Christianity, following the Council of Nicaea and the teachings of Paul, has traditionally asserted that there will be a bodily resurrection of the dead, and a physical, not merely spiritual, afterlife. This view appears to be incompatible with Spiritualism, where the merely spiritual existence is superior to the embodied one.

The Psychic and The 'Extra-Sense'

The mechanisms of perception are mainly involved in extracting statistical correlations from the world to create a model that is temporarily useful (Ramachandran, 1988)

In common parlance the word psychic is generally used to characterize a person who claims to have an ability to perceive information hidden from the normal senses through extrasensory perception (ESP), or who is said by others to have such abilities. Put another way, one who is capable of extraordinary mental processes and sensitive to supernatural influences or forces.

Extra-Sensory Perception as a phrase was adopted by Duke University psychologist J. B. Rhine in the 1950's to describe abilities such as telepathy, clairaudience, and clairvoyance, precognition (seeing the future) or retrocognition (non-direct awareness of past events).

Interestingly ESP is also sometimes casually referred to as a sixth sense, gut instinct or hunch or intuition. The term implies acquisition of information by means external to the basic limiting assumptions of science, which, amongst other things suggests that living organisms can only receive information from the past to the present – the way we perceive the passage of time (*times arrow*).

The key thing in all of the above is that 'information' which is unknown to the 'psychic' is obtained through means that are beyond (or outside) the range the five senses – seeing, hearing, feeling, tasting, smelling.

In ***Psi*** literature the range of extra-sensory (psychic) abilities include:-

Clairvoyance (from French clair meaning "clear" and voyance meaning "vision") which refers to the ability to gain information about an object, person, location or physical event through means other than the known human senses. The information can be said to be visual in nature so that the clairvoyant ("one who sees clearly") creates internal visual representations.

Clairsentience (feeling/touching) is the ability to acquire 'psychic' information primarily by feeling; by creating 'phsyical' representation. The word "clear" is from the French clair, and "sentience" is derived from the Latin sentire, "to feel".

Clairsentience is also one of the six human special functions mentioned or recorded in Buddhism. In this context it is regarded as an ability that can be obtained at advanced meditation level. Generally the term refers to a person who can feel the vibration of other people. There are many different degrees of clairsentience ranging from the perception of diseases of other people to the thoughts or emotions of other people.

Clairaudience (hearing/listening) again from late 17th century French clair (clear) and audience (hearing)] is a form of extra-sensory perception wherein a person acquires information through auditory representations.

So clairaudience is essentially the ability to hear in a paranormal manner, as opposed to paranormal seeing (clairvoyance) and feeling (clairsentience).

Clairaudience may refer not to actual perception of sound, but may instead indicate impressions of the "inner mental ear" similar to the way many people think words without having auditory impressions. But it may also refer to actual perception of sounds such as voices, tones, or noises which, some claim, are not apparent to other humans or to recording equipment

In Buddhism, it is believed that those who have extensively practiced Buddhist meditation and have reached a higher level of consciousness can activate their "third ear" and hear the music of the spheres; i.e. the music of the celestial gandharvas.

Clairalience (smelling) also known as clairescence. In the field of parapsychology, clairalience (or alternatively, clairolfactance) [presumably from late 17th century French clair (clear) and alience (smelling)] is a form of extra-sensory perception wherein a person accesses psychic knowledge through the physical sense of smell.

Claircognizance (knowing) presumably from late 17th century French clair (clear) and cognizance (possibly middle English cognisaunce or old French conoissance, knowledge) is where a person acquires psychic knowledge primarily by means of intrinsic knowledge. It is the ability to know something without a physical explanation why they know it.

Clairgustance (tasting) in which a 'psychic' is able to taste a substance without putting anything in their mouth. It is claimed that those who possess this ability are able to perceive the essence of a substance from the spiritual or ethereal realms through taste.

In all of the above we are really talking about 'extensions' to human senses in which there appears to be, or there are claims of, an ability to perceive things which are beyond the known ranges of human perception.

I find it interesting that in certain spiritual practices, Buddhism has already been mentioned, there is the notion that through practice, meditation and personal development, a person is able to improve and extend their perception so that other information, perhaps deeper meanings can be gained from an individuals' interaction with other people and the world (cosmos).

In James Cameron's movie Avatar, which is crammed full of spiritual references, not least the title of the movie itself, the forest dwelling peoples being colonized by the Skyfolk, speak the phrase 'I See You', which infers a knowledge or connection which is beyond the purely physical.

Like many of the references in this film we recognize the influence of the teachings of native peoples as well as direct references to Hindu mythology. The whole story is based upon the familiar stories of 'land rights' and 'exploitation' of first-nations peoples.

For me the clutter of extra-sensory and paranormal rhetoric is of less significance than the possibility that people can become more 'aware' and less governed by prejudicial dogma by being able to 'see' each other clearly. But then perhaps that's the humanist within me.

Back to Psychic talents which some purport to possess...

Many of the terms and phrases which have passed into everyday speak in relation to *ESP* and *Psychic Talents* were coined by the early researchers and authors.

Psychometry is related to clairsentience. This word appears to be derived from the words psyche and metric, and as such means "soul-measuring".

Pyrokinesis, which many claim to come from the Greek words pûr, meaning "fire, lightning" and and kínesis, meaning "motion"), seems to have been coined by horror novelist Stephen King for his 1980 novel, Firestarter.

Psychokinesis from the Greek "psyche", meaning mind, soul, spirit, heart, or breath; and "kinesis", meaning motion, movement; literally "mind-movement")

The word **Telekinesis** (in Greek literally "distant-movement") seems to be a synonym.

Describing mental movement or motion of solid matter, abbreviated as PK and TK respectively, it is a term coined by publisher Henry Holt to refer to the direct influence of mind on a physical system that cannot be entirely accounted for by the mediation of any known physical energy.

Precognition, (from the Latin præ-, "before," and cognitio, "acquiring knowledge"), has sometimes been called future sight, and second sight.

This type of extrasensory perception involves knowledge of future information that cannot be deduced from presently available and normally acquired sense-based information or laws of physics or nature. This awareness presenting as premonitions (from the Latin praemonēre) and can deal with information about future events which is perceived as an emotion.

Retrocognition (also known as postcognition), from the Latin retro meaning "backward, behind" and cognition meaning "knowing", describes "knowledge of a past event which could not have been learned or inferred by normal means". The term was coined by Frederic W. H. Myers the first president and founder of the Society for Psychical Research.

Telepathy (from the ancient Greek tele meaning "distant" and pathe or patheia meaning "feeling, perception, passion, affliction, experience") is the supposed transmission of

information from one person to another without using any of our known sensory channels or physical interaction.
Like retrocognition, the term was coined in 1882 by Frederic W. H. Myers has remained more popular than the earlier expression **thought-transference**.

527965176

If we look back at an earlier definition of the word 'psychic' we can see how all of the abilities above apply to the processing of *information* in the mind. Without getting too hung up at the moment on what we actually mean by information, it can be suggested that the ONLY difference between someone who is called a psychic and someone who is not is upon the limits (or boundaries) placed upon the sensory apparatus of the human being.

It is also worth noting that, in terms of proposed psychic abilities, there need not be any need to accept the philosophies of the spiritualist movement.

Mediums claim direct communication with 'spirits' inhabiting a 'spiritual world'. Their ability to obtain information from the spiritual realm is as much dependent upon the mediums claimed skills as it is on the willingness of the 'spirits' to communicate.

On the other hand many psychic abilities, or claimed psychic abilities, do not require an interaction with a spiritual realm, but are more about interactions between the individual and the universe they inhabit.

Ironically research into Mediumship and Psi is complicated not only by the need to create scientific protocols but also by the fact that any verifiable (or more correctly non-verifiable) information relayed by medium could have a psi (telepathic) source.

What separates the two possible sources (mind to mind or mind to spirit, if you like) lies within the belief systems to which the different practitioners adhere.

Human Senses

Your own body is a phantom, one that your brain has temporarily constructed purely for convenience.
(Ramachandran, 1988)

It is our senses which take information from the outside world, the physical world outside of self, which is then 'coded' through our perception to create patterns of meaning, relevance and representations of the 'the world out there' inside our minds (brains).

Our perception of the world is at least one step removed from the direct experience of our world since our senses fuel our perceptions.

Our understanding of the world is at least two steps removed from our direct experience of the world since it is our perceptions which drive our reactions, understandings and internal representations of the external world.

Whilst we often speak of the five senses of sight, sound, taste, touch and smell, the reality is a little more complex.

In fact human beings have a multitude of senses including...

Sight	(ophthalmoception)
Hearing	(audioception)
Taste	(gustaoception)
Smell	(olfacoception or olfacception)
Touch	(tactioception)
Temperature	(thermoception)
Kinesthetic sense	(proprioception)
Pain	(nociception)
Balance	(equilibrioception)
Acceleration	(kinesthesioception)
Time	(chronoception)

With such a list, and this is not exhaustive, it is worth noting that there is still much debate about what actually defines a sense, or an internal awareness and, more importantly for this discussion, how some of these inter-relate in the mind to create meaning from the chaos of sensory information in order to act within or upon ourselves and the world.

There are **two points** to be made here...

The **first** we know that other animals on this planet have sharper, more acute, finely tuned (discriminatory) senses than do we. In terms of the Sensory Olympics we are not in the premier league.

Imagine what the world smells like to a bloodhound. When we walk down the street, our senses tell us who's doing what at that moment but a bloodhound's nose allows it to perceive that same street across time – hence their ability to follow 'the scent'.

The Silvertip grizzly's sense of smell is seven times stronger than that of the bloodhound. Silvertips can smell fear, just like any other predator, but unlike most predators, they can smell your fear over distances of 18 miles.

Certain spiders have tetrachromatic vision. That means that where we see three primary colors, they see four – the fourth colour is ultraviolet.

There's a particular species of starfish that has calcite crystals embedded in its skin, surrounded by chromatophores (color-changing cells found in the octopus and cuttlefish as well) that allow it to not only change color in ways a chameleon would envy but also to control the amount of light passing into the calcite crystals.

These calcite crystals are tied to nerve bundles designed to detect light and are, in fact, formed into lenses. This makes the entire creature a single eye the size of an adults open hand.

7291011253

Each of the separate crystals acting together like the facets of a compound eye, their individual images combining to form a single clear picture; the light-collecting lenses focus light on the skeleton of the creature, which then redirects it to "windows" of clear material in the skeleton that focus the light onto the optic nerve bundles, which then relay the information to a ring of nerves around the central disc of the body.

Pigeons, as we know, have a kind of inbuilt GPS tracking system. Deposits of magnetite just above their beaks make their heads work like living, thinking compasses. In essence then they are sensitive to magnetic fields – magnetoperception.

Hammerhead Sharks have an enhanced ability to detect electric fields, and incidentally, better smell and a wider field of vision than most sharks, with 360 degrees of vertical binocular vision.

All sharks have receptors called ampullae of Lorenzini.

Hammerheads just have more of them, as a result, they can detect half a billionth of a volt.

By way of comparison, a static electric shock you may get from a personal combination of footwear, underwear and carpeting interacting with a grounding metal is around 8,000 to 10,000 volts of static. That is more than a trillion times the voltage the Hammerhead can sense.

The average human can see fire for hundreds if not thousands of feet and can possibly smell it for hundreds. Jewel beetles can sense a pine fire tens of miles away.

The decidedly odd Duckbilled Platypus possesses electroreception, the ability to sense electric fields generated by muscular contraction. That means they can sense muscle movement and be aware of the direction from which it came.

And, if that's not enough to put our sensory apparatus to shame it's worth thinking about the fact that the list above is the tip of the iceberg when it comes to the super-sense animals possess.

In comparison our senses of sight, hearing, touch, smell, and taste are extremely limited and can only respond to the small range of light, sound, tactile, olfactory, gustatory events.

Our senses receive limited information about the outside world.

The **second** point is to recognize the amount of sensory processing which goes on beneath the level of our conscious awareness.

The unconscious, or sub-conscious, mind processes sensory information making 'decisions' about what information to combine and in what ways in order to present an internal representation of the external world.

In essence we create personal realities based upon how we, as individuals, create meaning, value and importance from our perception of the outside world (remember our perception is at least one step removed from the 'real world experience').

Our brains are pattern matching and belief generating machines.

When sensory information is being processed the mind will try to associate the 'new information' with its past experience of similar information. It associates sensory information so as not to become overwhelmed and hence creates generalizations.

Past experience, expectation and beliefs can be considered as the templates the mind uses to categorize sensory input.

We know that perception can be fooled as a result of this process (think of optical illusions, the craft of the magician, internal hallucinations which appear to have an external source).

We know that this kind of perceptual shortcut has survival value – we associate the rustle of a bush in the dark with the sense of 'being on alert' since those of our ancestors who developed a survival 'instinct' did not get eaten by the sabre tooth tiger and lived on to pass their genes.

This begs an interesting question.

What happens to sensory based information that either is not understood, as in does not fit pre-existing patterns or current expectations, or is simply not presented to the conscious mind in terms of 'current awareness'?

Maybe this information is simply dismissed and then deleted.

Maybe it 'hangs around', is stored, waiting to be placed on a suitable hook in the treasury of *almost experienced experiences*.

We are incredibly selective about the kind of information we pay attention to.

In a very real sense attention goes where emotion flows so we are more likely to select information which has personal emotional relevance or personal investment to process.

Since we create meaning from experience, guided by expectation, then we can have rich internal worlds which, sometimes, are **inspired by** rather than being **reflections of** the external world.

Of course this means that by default we each of respond to and create at least two realities.

The first can be considered as the 'consensus reality'. This is the reality wherein we find truths we can share within our specific social groupings. Frequently within these groups there will be a shared vocabulary; a set of shared or at least agreed values and a belief system in which we can validate our experience of the world.

This 'consensus reality' may or may not conform to the objective reality of science wherein we can create systems of measurements, theories and hypotheses of universality as well as standardized tests about the nature of experience. In all senses this is the world in which the physical and mathematical sciences operate; the world in which scientific methodology can have reign.

There is also the subjective reality of the individual. The individual may apply some very personal rules about what can and cannot exist within this reality. They may adhere to a pragmatism which applies the variations of the objective measures used in the world of science or they may not.

In many ways this would be the home of the social scientist and psychologist who seeks to apply the rules and theories constructed in 'objective' reality in order to explore and explain the personal landscape of motivation, behaviour and belief.

Of course personal, subjective reality will also contain elements of the individuals' myth, experience and personal beliefs. There will be the choice as to whether the nature of personal reality and experience can be 'opened' up to objective assessment or not.

I frequently call myself a Rational Mystic in that I recognize that I am constructing a personal subjective reality in which I find relevance and meaning. However I am also willing to subject my experiences to objective measurement and exploration without feeling the need to diminish any personal relevance.

Such an attitude means, for me, that if someone tells me of a personal paranormal experience, for example, I am more than willing to talk about what it means for them and accept that experience and their interpretation of it was (and is) valid.

If, however, that same person wishes to insist that their, in this case paranormal experience, has meaning, value and a truth beyond their personal world I am more than willing to explore (objectively) their assumptions, perceptions and conclusions.

I short personal experiences can be shared and accepted, but as soon as those experiences are presented as evidence of truths beyond the individual then they are up for question, debate and challenge.

Levels of Reality

Scientific Reality

Everything is Objective

Observable, Measureable, Testable, Theories are Tentative

Psychic Reality

Everything is Subjective

Interpretation, Personal Resonance, 'Truth'

Shamanic Reality

Everything is Symbolic

Metaphor, Allegory, Signs, Portents, Omens

Mystical Reality

Everything is Everything

Relax – Don't Worry Be Happy

We can choose the realty in which we operate and learn about ourselves, each other and our inter-relationships.

(Jones, Ramblings of a Rational Mystic, 2011)

Of course each reality, each framework within which we create meaning, will become a consensus reality the moment we start to share it and find others who agree with the interpretations we have made.

So those who subscribe to, say, a spiritualist belief system, will find others to share their experience and have their experiences validated. The resulting consensus reality of shared understandings and vocabulary will continue to be self-referential and (possibly) cease to be objective and questioning. If such groups become isolated or isolationist (exclusive), then, there is the danger of cult-like behaviours developing.

I have written elsewhere of the nature of the skeptic, the cynic and the cult of anti-intellectualism, so will not repeat myself here suffice to say that the moment any individual or group becomes closed to question, debate, reflection and change, there is the potential of prejudice, bigotry and persecution.

Scientific, Spiritual, Skeptical, Mystical, Magical, Religious, Humanist individuals and groups can fall foul of being self-referential and closed to new ideas so sabotaging any of their initial ambitions of becoming 'enlightened', 'learned', 'inclusive' and 'collaborative'.

Knowledge, Belief and Truth

After spending some time talking about the need to ensure we can agree about the meaning of the words we use, I feel that it is important to ensure that I share something of what I mean by these three important words.

Knowledge - the 'facts' and 'ideas' we amass upon which we base our understanding of the world.

It is something that changes, develops, extends and evolves.

For some it is fixed, static and stable. Some will use the 'argument from tradition' to support views and opinions with the assumption that 'old' was 'less complicated' and somehow better. They forget that 'traditional ways' are based upon *what was 'known'* rather than *what is now 'known'*. Some Alternative Approaches to therapy and medicine have an approach which has not kept pace with scientific progress. One wonders if Samuel Hahnemann (1755–1843), the 'father of Homeopathy, would have changed his views in the light of what we now know about disease? At the time he was writing far less was known about disease mechanisms and, for his time, he was responding to what was known **then.**

I often smile to myself thinking about how the practices of Homeopathy (developed 1800's), Chiropractic (developed 1890's), Acupuncture (1003 and promoted widely 1683), Reflexology (systematically re-presented in 1913) would have been if those originating the systems had the benefit of 21st Century knowledge.

Does traditional mean better? This for me has to be the moderating question.

Belief - the assumptions, attitudes and ways we define and explain our experiences of the world.

Our beliefs shape our perceptions and our behaviours.
Beliefs are maintained by the evidence we have to support them. As explored earlier, our belief in Father Christmas was supported not only by the arrival of presents (or not) on Christmas morning, but also by the cultural stories, icons, symbols and behaviours.

It is only when we are invited to question the nature of the evidence being presented are we able to re-consider (possibly re-affirm) what we believe.

Neurologically our brains are pattern matching and belief creating machines.

We need to create beliefs about the world in order to function within it.

We need to recognize patterns in order to save time in re-processing and re-coding every experience.

Both of these functions of the brain are open to being fooled or confused – optical illusions, magicians and politicians being three examples of things which can test our observational and cognitive assumptions.

Truth - ultimately unknowable but is defined by Knowledge and Beliefs.

In many ways truth is matter of perspective; generally a matter of agreement and sometimes the rhetoric of oppression.

(Jones, Ramblings of a Rational Mystic, 2011)

But most remarkable of all are those ... who have deeply moving spiritual experiences, including a feeling of divine presence and the sense that they are in direct communion with God.

Everything around them is imbued with cosmic significance. They may say, "I finally understand what it's all about. This is the moment I've been waiting for all my life. Suddenly it all makes sense." Or, "Finally have insight into the true nature of the cosmos."

I find it ironic that this sense of enlightenment, this absolute conviction that Truth is revealed at last, should derive from limbic structures concerned with emotions rather than from the thinking, rational parts of the brain that take so much pride in their ability to discern truth and falsehood.

Could it be that human beings have actually evolved specialized neural circuitry for the sole purpose of mediating religious experience? The human belief in the supernatural is so widespread in all societies all over the world that it's tempting to ask whether the propensity for such beliefs might have a biological basis.

(Ramachandran, 1988)

Back to 'Psychic Development'

I don't need to be psychic to feel you thinking – *what's this go to do with psychic development?*

Once we start to think about the restrictions of our senses; the limitations we place on our understandings of the world and the idea that 'reality' is flexible then we can start to think about the nature of personal perception and challenge some of our thoughts about reality and how we share our realities with others.

As you will see I am not necessarily arguing for the need for having extra-sensory perception in order to extend personal intuition in ways that approach the skills claimed by psychics. I am suggesting that developing clarity of thought, the ability to really connect with others and a sense of a personal relationship with the Cosmos, for want of a better term, is the journey all mystics, spiritual teachers and humanists have been promoting.

If a 'psychic' is an individual who is able to **integrate sensory** experience and intuition in such a way as to perceive the world in different, possibly unique ways then an understanding of how we create meaning and have limited perception is a starting point.

In many ways we all have a kind of arrogance when it comes to the way we process sensory information. Unless we know an individual has a sensory impairment then we can all too often assume that what we see is what they see; what they hear is what we hear and so on.

In conversation with others we may speak of the blue carpet and red chair and since they acknowledge the existence of both we can assume they are seeing what we see.

Putting aside the question as to how do we know that 'their blue' is 'our blue' and 'their red' is 'our red' there are other questions as to what 'blueness' and 'redness' looks, sounds, feels, thinks, smells and tastes like.

It has been suggested that some 12% of the population are 'synaesthetic'.

A synaesthete is a person whose 'sensory modalities' are crossed to some degree.

No doubt you have heard of people who see numbers or sounds as colours and may have thought that this was simply a matter of learned association.

However the neurologist Ramachandran (Ramachandran, 1988) has shown that such experiences and cross-over sensations are neurological, that is to do with brain wiring.

I have worked with a young person who was a sound-taste synasthete. This meant that each sound produced a taste experience. He was literally tasting words and some words had a bad taste. In groups the clash of tastes and sounds were overwhelming and he would start to 'gag' and feel physically sick.

There are some neurologists who state that we are all born with synaesthetic abilities and that during early brain development (between the ages of 1 – 5 when neurological connections are being 'pruned') this ability vanishes. Other researchers have suggested that this ability is crucial in terms of acquisition of language – when the child learns to speak. They cite the existence of cross-sensory language (that looks sharp : that sounds rough) and note the fact that young children interact with their world by touching, tasting, feeling, smelling as well as seeing.

What matters here is the idea that individual responses to the external world and the sensory information it provides is unique and our ability to recognize this increases our openness to the reality of others.

Every experience we experience is a result of the way the brain interprets what we see, hear, feel, taste, touch, smell and think.

These processes give rise to an inner sense of 'mind'.

Often brain and mind are used interchangeably but in the strictest possible sense BRAIN is the biological structure inside our heads and MIND is the collection of processes it drives.

Whilst some people like to think of 'mind' as being somehow separate and different to the brain, and therefore consciousness relating to something esoteric and distinct (the basis of spiritual thinking perhaps), most neurologists seem to accept that Mind and Consciousness are emergent properties of brain processes.

This idea is not, however, what I wanted to talk about here...

It seems that as each month passes scientists who ask questions about the brain are making more and more sense of what is one of the most complex systems known.

We know that if the living brain is 'stimulated' with small electrical charges (electricity is the language of the brain) the person will experience some very real sensations.

Such sensations can include:-

- a 'feeling' that there is some 'higher self'
- a 'god-like presence',
- 'otherworldly entity' in contact with the individual
- a sense that the individuals own consciousness is outside of itself and looking down upon the 'body'
- hearing sounds
- seeing shapes, shadows, patterns, flashing lights, people recalling memories and the associated feelings

All of these are REAL to the individuals concerned - they are genuine personal experiences.

Of course this research must have implications for any and all paranormal investigations. However powerful and personally relevant these experiences are for the individual (and this is where my mystical/transpersonal psychology interests lie) the fact of the matter is that all personal experiences are the result of personal brain processing.

Now before I get too many comments saying what about 'shared' experiences, I have to say that the mechanisms for individuals sharing a 'reality' bring into play some other powerful social-psychological process that need to be explored before we can simply accept as 'real' any jointly witnessed paranormal event.

What are these possible social-psychological processes?

Well they could include confabulation, mass-hysteria, social compliance, mass hallucination, misperception, misrecognition, spiritual rapture, *hypnotic* effects (which could be all of the above) as well as environmental conditions that are conducive to any or all of the above - infrasound, weather conditions ... and so on.

Back to the brain; it can be demonstrated that stimulating the brain in specific areas will produce internal sensations that are **real** from the individual's perspective.

The mystical experience begins, perhaps, with the brain and then is given personal meaning, understanding and relevance by the individuals culture, beliefs, desires, hopes and dreams,

So the first step of any form or personal, psychic or spiritual development is to ask yourself some soul-searching questions about the degree to which you are open to the worlds of others; the flexibility of your belief systems; your willingness to accept that some of your experiences of the world may have been the product of mis-perception and a desire to celebrate personal realities as well as appreciate the potential limitations of the realities shared by you and others; that *consensus reality* that can produce dogmatism and a sense of 'owning the truth'.

1459437077

Transpersonal Psychology

Transpersonal psychology is a school of psychology that studies the transpersonal, self-transcendent or spiritual aspects of the individual human experience.

Transpersonal experiences can be considered as "experiences in which the sense of identity or self extends beyond (trans) the individual or personal to encompass wider aspects of humankind, life, psyche or cosmos – in essence what many may call a 'mystical experience'.

We have already seen that for many neurologists there is the generalized view that all experiences are not only based within the brain, but created by it. Richard Dawkins, like many other scientists have conceded that the brain is 'wired' to accept and create religious experiences and so there is possibly a evolutionary advantage to having a belief is some kind of omnipresent 'overseer', particularly in relation to the development of social mores and values.

The Journal of Transpersonal Psychology offers the following definition:-

... {transpersonal psychology } *"is concerned with the study of humanity's highest potential, and with the recognition, understanding, and realization of unitive, spiritual, and transcendent states of consciousness"* (Lajoie, 1992)

Now even if we accept that 'feelings' and 'awareness of' 'higher spiritual realms' and conversations with 'God' are experiences which the brain creates, this does not mean that there can be no learning or self-development to be drawn from them. Indeed one of the challenges Transpersonal Psychologists face is the reality that their academic conversations about the nature of these experiences can, and have been hi-jacked by some who wish to promote a very specific spiritual (religious) agenda.

It seems that sometimes the desire to box and hence limit some exciting avenues for debate is a trend within certain modern New Age approaches.

In some cases the integration of philosophical and academic approaches within revivalist spiritual movements (neo-paganism, New Age Philosophies, revisionings of traditional/ancient healing practices etc) can allow for dynamic debate, but in many cases the inclusion of ideas from humanistic psychology, transpersonal approaches and other natural sciences leads to confusion (at best) and fraudulent claims (at worst).

Consider, for example, the complex ideas within what we now know as Quantum Physics being cherry-picked, mis-represented and used as 'marketing labels' within alternative therapies.

Transpersonal Psychology deals with issues and ideas which are at the core of personal, subjective, spiritual experience and as such is rife for misappropriation by 'gurus' wishing to promote their particular brand of spiritual doctrine (dogma).

I was recently reading through some notes left by a spiritual teacher in a room I was working in. The worksheet being given to students offered 'Ten Spiritual Truths' which were not being presented as presuppositions upon which to inspire debate, but as 'rules' and 'universal truths' which **must** be accepted in order to develop personally, spiritually and as a 'psychic'.

Many of these "rules", I recognized as being direct 'lifts' from 'Occult' texts and European re-workings of Eastern 'mystical teaching' created during the Renaissance. The same texts of course were the basis for magical orders like The Golden Dawn, The Rosicrucian's and later the Theosophists. However even these older, derivative, sources were honorable enough to make some allusion to pre-existing texts, whereas this list of 'laws' had no provenance, other than that of the spiritual teacher; misrepresented some of those earlier 'ideas' as definitive laws and rules AND supported some of them with hurried, misunderstood and overly popularized pseudo-science masquerading as 'real scientific fact'.

3471897693

In short this particular guru was feeding 'seekers' with rules rather than inspiring questions; laws rather than provocations and truths rather than possibilities.

It is one thing, surely, to make statements against which students can test their thoughts and from which debate can be inspired and another to 'tell 'em how it really is!"

I guess I should repeat my earlier caveat...

Everything I write in this book is a statement of my current understanding and offered as a set of statements against which you, dear reader, can vent your spleen and challenge your thinking. My aim is to provoke, offer ideas and opinion and articulate presuppositions which, may sound like rules and laws, but are merely summaries of possibility.

Total Sensory Perception

I want to make these statements of PERSONAL TRUTH or BELIEF here.

Psychic – Intuitive Readings have a real value for most of the people who seek them

If the 'reader' is coming from a space of support and empowerment the value is greater

For the most part it may not matter if the Psychic, Medium, Intuitive can prove their abilities to the scientific community.

Pseudo-Sceptics (those who set out to debunk rather than question) are closed minded

New Age Space Cadets (those who accept without question) are, in an odd way, also closed minded

Psychic Fraud is a reality as are those who profit from the need, pain and dependence of others.

I think that's clear?

To take things a step further...

In order to set the record straight I need to make it clear that I have given 'readings', do 'readings' and will probably continue to do 'readings' – and I do work in Mind Body and Spirit fairs from time to time and run talks, workshops and sessions on many topics that would be familiar to with those who enjoy the mystical/spiritual side of things.

However I make no claims of psychic ability *in the way that some think of such skills*, and in many ways I feel these claims are simply part of the marketing label some folks use (require).

5493257219

I have studied the Tarot (I had my first deck over 40 years ago); I have read into and worked with Numerology, Astrology, and Palmistry amongst other so called divinatory 'arts'.

They are interesting **symbolic systems** and although they (may) have no scientific validity (in an objective, measurable way) it is clear that they have a personal resonance on a subjective and hence formative level.

A 'reading' as defined by most would refer to a situation where an individual (the client) receives insightful information from a 'reader' who is using some psychic, intuitive, mediumistic or symbolic system.

The 'reader' acts as a listener, confident, advisor and perhaps councilor (in the broadest sense).

The 'client' receives 'information' from a third party who is removed from their own personal situation and can offer 'insights'

In this situation all things being equal there is no need to demonstrate scientifically the reality of any claim made by the reader as the assessment is being made by the client as to the relevance and value of the information.

It matters little if that information is vague; comes from spirit; personal insights or messages in the sand – and if it does matter then this is either in the mind of the person giving the reading or in the type of reader preferred by the client.

I have never liked the notion of 'reading' since the process for me is always about a conversation, a dialogue in which the 'intuitions' of the reader based upon whatever system they use are part of a transformational process. (Jones, Transformational Readings, 2012)

Here is a question?

Are the readings being given by the multitude of readers out there 'transformational' in any way?

Do they ask the 'client' to explore and reflect upon their situation and their own inner world or are they simply vehicles for the 'reader' to show off their 'spiritual prowess' and own 'advancement'?

Does the reading become a monologue with the reader seeking 'proof' of connection in some way or is the reading a dialogue, a conversation around which images, ideas, emotions are discussed?

I am afraid I see a lot of the former and less of the latter.

Some of the psychological issues related to this kind of reading (where the 'reader' tells) is that the client can have a sense of **'disempowerment'** and this of course will lead to an **abdication of personal responsibility.**

Apologies if that does sound a little 'fluffy', but in a very real sense we can all be changed by the conversations we have and in the situation of a 'psychic reading' the potential for impact-full dialogue is great.

A Psychic is …. ???

To re-iterate what I said earlier…

"Psychic is a much used term and one that immediately creates in the mind of the listener certain presuppositions. The word itself comes from the Greek word psychikos which means "of the soul" or "mental".

785381909978

This was an attempt to make it clear that when I used the word 'psychic' it was in the sense of attempting to create deeper understandings and meaning through the integration and use of all of the senses.

I argue against the idea of 'extra-sensory' perception in favour of 'total sensory' perception. In this usage of the term the 'psychic' attempts to become open to all of the conscious and unconscious information available so as to communicate clearly and effectively.

In any situation there will be an overwhelming amount of information which overloads our senses and only a fraction of which we will pay conscious attention to.

In terms of conscious processing there is a kind of 'magic number' – that number is 7 plus or minus 2. (Miller, 1956)

In essence we can only pay conscious attention to between 5 and 9 'chunks' of information – anything above this threshold tends to be processed below the 'level of consciousness'. This means that some kind of filtering of information must be happening unconsciously and there are 'choices being made' as to what requires our conscious attention.

As a general rule **'attention goes' where 'emotion flows'**, so those things we have decided are important are the things we to which we give attention.

Many esoteric traditions celebrate the practice of meditation in some form to some degree. The practice of focusing conscious attention and shifting attention allows for 'clear seeing' – clairvoyance.

To be 'open' to different kinds of sensory information whilst removing any presuppositions; expectations and generalizations is a worthy goal to achieve. It is not an easy one however since every aspect of conscious thought is directed and filtered by our preconceptions, beliefs and prejudices.

Total Sensory Perception – Person 2 Person

Inter-Personal Communication

People like to think they are good listeners; in fact 'active listening' is a skill which many believe they have mastered when in effect their journey towards that destination has merely just begun.

It is worth considering the idea that in any person-to-person communication is really about eight 'personalities'.

For the person who is speaking there is:-

a) What they are saying
b) What they mean
c) How they want to be perceived
d) How they are being perceived

For the person who is listening there is:-

a) What they hear
b) What they understand
c) How they want to be perceived
d) How they are being perceived

Our personal agenda in a conversation will become a block to effective listening; our prejudices and beliefs will be projected onto the substance of what we hear and how we understand another person's actions, needs and desires.

In short 'being present' in a situation requires us to become open to what can be understood rather than what we need to understand.

聽 YOU
EYES
EARS
HEART
UNDIVIDED
ATTENTION

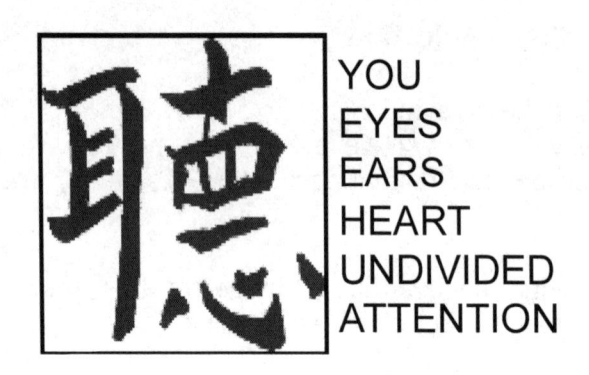

We know that such pictograms are combined of other elements and this one really emphasises the nature active listening.

As a listener YOU use your EYES to see what the speaker is saying; your EARS to hear their words; your HEART to show empathy and hence connect to their world and UNDIVIDED ATTENTION to let them know you are 'with them'.

The most challenging of these in most cases will be the 'giving' of your 'undivided attention'. Setting aside our own needs to be heard; the desire to let others know some part of our personal story is the issue.

In a conversation we are hearing what is being said; planning an appropriate response and seeking to move forward with an (unconscious?) agenda. As such our emotions ensure that we pay conscious, close attention to only those things which interest or challenge us. Our perception is narrowed and so too our awareness – our clarity.

Stepping outside of our personal agenda, allowing our attention to focus entirely on the speaker increases our perceptual field so that we are aware of other subtle cues and shifts which add to the understanding of the meaning we are gleaning from what we are hearing.

By allowing our attention to include how something is said as well as considering what is said increases our understanding. Normally our 'unconscious mind' deals with the subtleties of how something is said and communicates its findings with a sense of 'connection', 'rapport' or 'congruence' however having some conscious idea the kind of things our unconscious mind processes allows for 'direction of attention' to things which will broaden our perception.

Tone of Voice

Not simply the way something is said, but the emphasis placed on words within a phrase.

"Well I said I want something done **now**!"

May mean or suggest something different to ...

"Well I said I **want** something done now!"

In the first case there is not only an implied command or demand for action but a statement of immediacy.

In the second the emphasis could be seen to be on the emotional need to be met rather than a call for immediate action.

What about ...

"Well I said I want **something** done now!"

This emphasis may suggest a lack of clarity about just what can be done to meet the need (want) for action.

Such emphases may come in the form of a shift in tone of voice, a change in pace or pattern of speech and even a gesture.

Being aware of the potential focus of the speaker's statement of need could allow for different questions or statements which extend the rapport.

For example

"Well I said I want something done **now**!"

Response:

OK, let's see what can be done immediately

"Well I said I **want** something done now!"

Response:

Ok, I sense that this situation really moves you and is about your needs at the moment

"Well I said I want **something** done now!"

Response:

Fine, what can be done now?

Whilst this all sounds really obvious, responding to the sub-text of another person's comment communicates the desire to understand, be-present and support.

Sensory Based Language

Consider the possibility that the following statements, which refer to the same thing, actually give clues to the way an individual is thinking about a situation.

"I **see** what you mean"

"I **hear** what you are saying"

"I **get** the **point**"

"I **understand** now"

To the superficial listener these phrases mean the same thing – but to an active listener they **imply** different things.

The SEE statement suggests that the listener is creating 'pictures' in their mind.

The HEAR statement suggests that the listener is replaying or relying on the sense they make of the words.

The GET THE POINT statement suggests that the listener has made an internal connection through 'feelings'

The UNDERSTAND statement suggests that the listener has connected the 'new ideas' with what they already know and have considered it fully.

This idea of sensory based language comes from a discipline known to some as Neuro-Linguistic Programming (NLP) and superficially seems a little trite. However the notion that we create internal representations of external realities has been discussed above and is philosophically a sound proposition.

The NLP idea that we have a *lead sensory processing system,* or way of creating internal 'maps', is interesting and hence worth considering.

358314549

If I am listening to the way someone expresses an idea or phrases a question I may get a sense of how best to respond.

So if someone says 'I don't see it', I will use visual language and words to help them create a 'brighter picture' in their mind.

If someone says 'I don't get it,' I will use kinesthetic (touch/feely) words to help them 'get in touch with' the ideas.

If that same person says "That doesn't sound right to me!" I will use different words, or changes in how I speak to restate the issue, point or question.

If they say "I don't understand', I may simply create a 'space' form them to think about the ideas and little more and encourage them to connect, associate or explore intellectually what has been said.

This system of language patterning requires more than the few words I have shared here, but for now consider what might happen if you actually paid such detailed attention to the way another person described their internal reality, thoughts and ideas.

If a person uses a lot of 'see' language then build pictures for them...

If a person uses a lot of 'hear' language then give words and phrases musicality...

If a person uses a lot of 'feel' language then explore emotions, connections, feelings and intuitions

If a person uses a lot of 'understand' or 'thinking' language then create space for them to 'internally process' what is being or has been said.

Words Which May Suggest Ways of Thinking

SEE	HEAR	FEEL	THINK
Bright	Loud	Point	Understand
Clear	Tone	Sense	Conclude
Picture	Pitch	Intuit	Reflect
Fuzzy	Volume	Sharp	Consider
Focus	In-Tune	Feel	Analyze
Colourful	Hear	Connected	Think

Body Language

We can think of Body Language in two ways.

There is the Macro-Body Language of gesture and body position about which numerous books have been written. Whilst it is true that such body language gives hints and clues as to the meaning behind the words we use care must be taken about over generalizations.

All body language 'experts' will agree that whilst there are patterns of unconscious behaviour which can suggest internal states, care must be taken to ensure that the 'reader' of physical language does not 'jump' to conclusions. The real secret is in looking for changes (or not) in posture rather than, for example, assuming that folded arms always mean 'defensiveness'.

I find micro-body language of more interest and worthy of attention. NLP practitioners make much mention of what they call 'eye accessing cues'.

Simply put when people are thinking their eyes will move. This was first noted in the 1940's and the idea seemed to be that an individual's eye-movement patterns offered clues to the kind of thinking that was being engaged in.

With the 'birth of NLP' the founders (or shall we say 'compilers' of what we now know as NLP) suggested that there was a specific pattern to these movements and could be considered thusly:-

The Content Of The Model: The Representational System

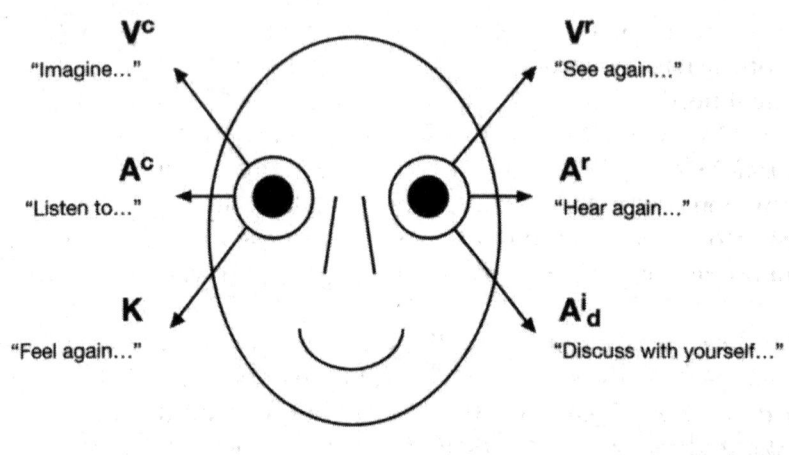

V^c — "Imagine..."
V^r — "See again..."
A^c — "Listen to..."
A^r — "Hear again..."
K — "Feel again..."
A^i_d — "Discuss with yourself..."

(Young, 1999)

The 'model' suggests that when people LOOK UP or stare straight ahead in a slightly defocused way, they are engaging in visual thinking.

If they look from side to side then they are engaging in auditory, sound processing, and if they down they are processing internal information.

The 're-presentational system' (as in re presenting information) model also suggests that...

Looking up to the right (as you look at the speaker) suggests they are 'recalling' visual information (remembering) and looking to the left is 'creating' or 'constructing' visual information.

The same pattern is suggested as being true for auditory processing – to the right recalling what has been heard and to the left 'constructing' words, sentences and sounds.

Looking down to the right (as you look at the speaker) suggests 'internal dialogue' (self-talk) and looking down to the left suggests 'going into feelings or emotions'.

Now this is a **MODEL** and not a fact.

Really look at people when they are talking and notice how their eyes are moving. The patterns suggested above may appear to hold true for the person you are looking at; the patterns may be reversed... there may be no discernible pattern...

The fact that **you are giving total attention**, briefly without staring and causing the speaker to feel interrogated, will actually improve your listening skills.

If you look back at the sensory language we explored earlier you will see that there is a link between the language patterns and the suggested 'eye access' cues. What I find interesting is that hand and arm gestures often follow a similar pattern – that is up when accessing visual information and down when accessing feelings.

There also seems to be a pattern to breathing and general posture which we can relate to these small (micro) body language clues.

Thought Process	Posture	Breathing	Gestures
SEE (V)	Leaning back, head tilted up, hands behind head...	High in chest, fast and shallow	Moving quickly; 'drawing' the object or events... pointing to specific locations in space related to particular times or emotional states...
HEAR (A)	Sitting upright, head tilted to side	Middle of chest, regular and moderate	Moving smoothly, conducting or demonstrating rhythm of speech; punctuation
FEEL (K)	Sitting forwards, head tilted down	Low in stomach, deep and slow	Relatively still, often in lap or clasped. May make 'grabbing' clutching gestures... Touching body frequently
THINK (T)	Head tilted to one side; may look pensive... possibly pursing lips in contemplation...	Even, similar to K, but may alternate between all positions as various chunks of information are processed...	Generally still... as if waiting... on hold.... May sigh and start as if to initiate something then pause...

Table : Rep Systems

If there is any truth in this 'construct' then it seems reasonable to suggest that these cues are things which we learn very early in our development and they become the things in which we develop unconscious competence.

We do not think about 'reading' these cues, we just do it.

That means, of course, when we stop to think about these processes and break them down into conscious steps, they can feel clumsy, awkward and (as more than one self-professed medium has said to me) 'all far too clever for them'.

Isn't that an interesting idea that **'unconscious neurological responses'** are 'too clever' for the medium who made the comment.

So what is the subtext here?

Is it that if they accept the possibility that such subtle forms of non verbal communication exists then it calls into question the source of the information they share when they are giving readings?

If this is the case then what follows may be even more threatening to their world view.

Micro-Expressions

Micro-expressions are the brief and involuntary facial expressions shown on human faces which result from the emotions they are experiencing.

The psychologist Paul Ekman believes that facial expressions are universal rather than culturally determined and has conducted numerous studies exploring this idea.

He has developed systems like the FACS, Facial Action Coding System, EMFACS, Emotion Facial Action Coding System from his research. If you have ever seen the TV series Lie to Me then you are familiar with Ekman's work.

9549325792

In the television series the 'body language expert' (played by Tim Roth) is well versed in the 'science of micro-expressions'. Paul Ekman actually advised on the series so, despite some artistic license, the abilities displayed by the Tim Roth character are those Ekman can demonstrate and claims he can teach others.

These micro-expressions are the merest 'flash' of an expression and last no more than one-tenth of a second.

This means that to catch-them in 'real time' requires a high degree of sensory acuity. I again would maintain that this acuity is part and parcel of our unconscious processing and filters. We are not consciously aware of seeing these emotional flashes, but if we are self-aware, we 'feel' them or have a sense about the reality of what someone is saying to us, for example.

Ekman suggests that there are seven universal emotions. These are:-

- **Disgust**
- **Anger**
- **Fear**
- **Sadness**
- **Happiness**
- **Surprise**
- **Contempt**

According to Paul Ekman each of these has a specific facial expression which is universal and can be described. It's no surprise that these seven emotions are emotions which we can recognise when we see others who are experiencing them.

An expression of 'disgust' can be easily imagined by most as can expressions of 'fear', 'sadness' and so on...

What Ekman suggests is that even if we try to mask these feelings in larger, possibly rehearsed, expressions the real emotional response would be 'flashed' before the covering 'mask' expression is formed.

So, in a social situation, the listener may want to be accepted by others and so measure (mask) their underlying feelings (emotions) related to what the speaker is saying BUT the micro-expression will indicate what they really feel or think.

In a group an affable person may be 'holding court' and perhaps being a little too loud. Everyone might be laughing at the guests antics, but the micro-expressions which flash when people look at the person who is the centre of attention, will expose the feelings that lie beneath the laughter.

Whilst others may not see the micro-expression they may well 'sense' the incongruity between the 'outer laugh' and the 'inner contempt'.

Ekman's work is controversial, however, if you look at the way people speak to each other; gaze at TV interviews with the sound off; look at photographs of people who publically agree yet privately disagree, I am sure you will notice these expressions; eye access and body language cues.

This kind of behavioural profiling is something we all do, generally unconsciously, and it allows us to have 'feelings' or a 'sense' about the honesty, congruence and even personality of others. We don't think about it – we create 'first impressions' and respond accordingly.

The sad fact is that there are many who find it difficult to revise their first impressions; in the same way as there are those who will not review beliefs in the light of new information; and such folk will find 'total sensory perception' difficult to achieve since their emotional responses are getting in the way.

1673033659

Paul Ekman's Seven Universal Emotions

FEAR   CONTEMPT   DISGUST

ANGER   SADNESS   HAPPINESS   SURPRISE

Virginia Satir

Virginia's Wisdom

(26 June 1916 - 10 September 1988)

We must not allow other people's limited perceptions to define us

Problems are not the problem; coping is the problem.

Life is not what it's supposed to be. It's what it is. The way you cope with it is what makes the difference.

I believe the greatest gift I can conceive of having from anyone is to be seen by them, heard by them, to be understood and touched by them

We need 4 hugs a day for survival. We need 8 hugs a day for maintenance. We need 12 hugs a day for growth.

Over the years I have developed a picture of what a human being living humanely is like. She is a person who understands values and develops her body, finding it beautiful and useful; a person who is real and is willing to take risks, to be creative, to manifest competence, to change when the situation calls for it, and to find ways to accommodate to what is new and different, keeping that part of the old that is still useful and discarding what is not

Communication Patterns – Satir Categories

People tend to use one of five patterns of language behaviour, according to Dr. Virginia Satir.

BLAMING: Blamers pepper their speech with words like: Always, Never, Nothing, Nobody, Everything, None, Not once (e.g. "You ALWAYS do EVERYTHING wrong!")

When they ask questions, they put an abnormally heavy stress on the question word – "WHY did you do that?" "WHEN will you start thinking of someone other than yourself?"

There are Blamers who are a bit less obvious.

For every Blamer who says "You idiot, don't you ever look where you're going?" others are more covert "Sweetheart, couldn't you be more careful where you put your feet just once in a while?"

Their body language is threatening.

They lean over you, shake their index finger or fist at you and scowl, frown or glare.

PLACATING: Placaters are almost the exact opposite of Blamers. They wiggle, fidget and lean; they hang on you, or cringe away from you. They are desperate to please and will not say what they want.

"Oh, you know me, whatever you want is okay with me!" "You know how I am, nothing bothers me."

COMPUTERS: They are determined to give the impression that they have no emotions, so they use very little body language, few facial expressions, few gestures.

They avoid the words "I, me, mine, you, yours", etc. to keep their language as divorced from the real world situation as possible.

"There is clearly no reason for alarm."
"It would appear there is a minor problem."

DISTRACTERS: Give the impression of linguistic chaos and panic. Under stress they cycle through the other patterns of blaming, placating, computing randomly and their body language is as disorganized as their words.

"Why don't you ever ask me what I'd like to do on the weekend? Not that it matters...you know how I am, anything that makes you happy. But simple courtesy would seem to indicate that the desires of both individuals be taken into account. But whatever you want is okay with me, you know."

LEVELERS: These are hard to spot because they may use the same words as a Blamer, Placater or Computer but there is a striking difference. S/He means exactly what he says.

There is no mismatch among the Leveler's words, body language or feelings.

When a Blamer says "Why do you always eat so much junk food?" it is a verbal attack; a Leveler who uses the same words may be impolite and unkind but the question is not an attack. There is no Blamer body language and no abnormal stress on words - it is a simple request for information.

Once you have identified which of the 5 modes you are dealing with in confrontations especially you can work to calm a situation, a judgment, a perception and a ask a 'transformational question'.

Here are the 'rules' for engaging with the different modes:-

Except for Leveling at a Leveler, try not to match the Satir mode coming at you. This will only intensify the confrontation.

If you don't know what to do, go to the Computer mode and maintain it. It is the most neutral mode and therefore will clash less than any other choice. From that position you can then make a choice as to how best to respond in the interaction.

Satir suggested that there is often incongruency between what a person's physiology communicates and what one actually feels inside.

She suggested that a Blamer, whilst adopting a controlling posture may be hiding a feeling of loneliness or lack of success...

A Placater may say with their body 'helplessness' and may feel 'worthless'...

A Computer 'calm and collected' may feel "uncomfortable" and "vulnerable"...

A Distracter may act like a 'scatterbrain' and feel 'uninvolved' or 'unloved'.

DEGREE of CONGRUENCE

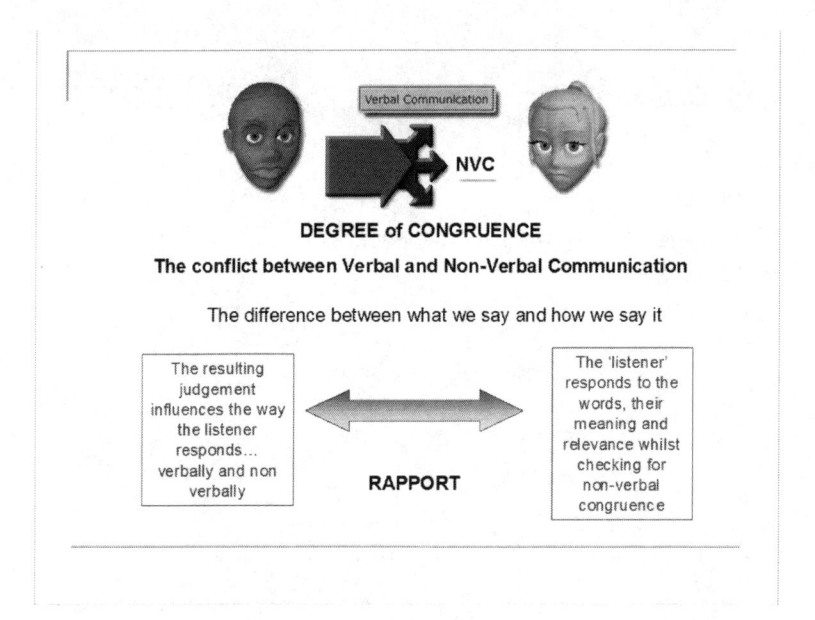

The conflict between Verbal and Non-Verbal Communication

The difference between what we say and how we say it

| The resulting judgement influences the way the listener responds... verbally and non verbally | **RAPPORT** | The 'listener' responds to the words, their meaning and relevance whilst checking for non-verbal congruence |

Stress and emotion pushes us out of 'leveler mode' and into one of the other categories.

Satir suggested that most people have learned to feel comfortable in their preferred category but that may be a poor way of coping as it reduces their choices and flexibility.

Satir Categories

PLACATOR

WORDS – agree "What ever you want is ok"

BODY – appeases

SELF-IMAGE – I'm not as important

Satir Categories

BLAMER

WORDS – disagree "You never get it right!"

BODY – accuses

SELF-IMAGE – I'm the boss

Satir Categories

COMPUTER
WORDS – ultra-reasonable "If one were to observe..
BODY – computes
SELF-IMAGE – I'm need to be in control

Satir Categories

DISTRACTOR
WORDS – irrelevant
BODY angular
SELF-IMAGE – Why am I here, am I relevant ?

Syntonic Listening

Is listening which is characterized by a high degree of emotional responsiveness to the environment.

When people are speaking - no matter how trivial the subject - their blood pressure rises; when people are listening, really listening and not just hearing, their blood pressure falls.

However, 'defensive' listeners, those who are just waiting on the edge of their chair for the chance to speak, rehearsing what they are going to say in their heads, struggling to interrupt, do not show a drop in blood pressure - it stays elevated just as if they were speaking.

People start to listen with the best of intentions, then realize they haven't heard a word the speaker was saying for some time.

This will happen no matter what the subject is.

If it's something that interests them, they stop listening because they want to be the one talking; if it's something that doesn't interest them, they will stop listening because they are bored.

To break this habit, it's necessary to drag the mind back when you catch it wandering and LISTEN.

When you catch yourself interrupting, stop, apologize, ask the speaker to continue and LISTEN.

Again, I can almost hear some of you saying – so, when are you going to get to the 'psychic development' bit?

Well, we're almost there.

To understand the idea of 'total sensory perception' I think it is necessary to have some idea as to the nature of the non-verbal communication which drives our initial understandings and reactions to someone else.

More importantly perhaps is the idea that these self same processes (if you like behavioural programmes) actually shape how **you** are being understood by others.

In reading the previous pages were you able to see, hear, feel and think about yourself and your own patterns?

The reality is, as far as I am currently aware, that the different processing styles (representational systems of Seeing, Hearing, Feeling and Thinking); the different ways of dealing with confrontations (as defined by Satir) are not labels of classification but are totally context dependent.

Our reactions to the outside world, the other people in it and our resulting behaviours are the result of internal processes which are often only at the edge of our awareness (if at all).

Attempting to explore your own unconscious communication patterns is, I would maintain, the first step in improving your communication with others and hence your 'total sensory perception'.

In doing so, you will be able to measure and reconsider your reactions so becoming more flexible and open in any situation.

Intuition

I find it amusing when I read some academic texts on aspects of the paranormal and note a tendency to 'lump together' psychic experiences under the banner of intuition.

Just what is this thing called intuition which seems to have a considerable amount of sway in our own decision making processes (all of which come from an emotional place)?

Intuition is often expressed as a 'gut feeling' a 'sense of knowing' or 'seeing that something is (or is not quite) right'.

If you've followed my thinking so far then you can't help but notice the 'sensory' language used to describe 'intuition'.

I define intuition as the sum total of the sensory experience, memories, associations, emotions and situations which are processed by my unconscious and presented as some kind of 'knowing' or 'sense' to my conscious mind.

But that then begs a question...

If intuition comes from the blending of my past experiences, learning, emotions and cultural references how can it be that sometimes connections and 'intuitive information' seems to have a source that is beyond my experience and knowing?

I would heartily recommend Malcolm Gladwell's book Blink for a 'rational' discussion of what he terms 'rapid cognition'.

As he writes:-

> It's a book about rapid cognition, about the kind of thinking that happens in a blink of an eye. When you meet someone for the first time, or walk into a house you are thinking of buying, or read the first few sentences of a book, your mind takes about two seconds to jump to a series of conclusions. Well, "Blink" is a book about those two seconds, because I think those instant conclusions that we reach are really powerful and really important and, occasionally, really good.
>
> You could also say that it's a book about intuition, except that I don't like that word. In fact it never appears in "Blink." Intuition strikes me as a concept we use to describe emotional reactions, gut feelings--thoughts and impressions that don't seem entirely rational. But I think that what goes on in that first two seconds is perfectly rational. It's thinking--its just thinking that moves a little faster and operates a little more mysteriously than the kind of deliberate, conscious decision-making that we usually associate with "thinking."
>
> (Gladwell)

Like Gladwell, I think that intuition is a rational, understandable process but is one which holds a good deal of emotional leverage. Where we possibly part company is when it comes to a consideration of a possible 'transpersonal' component of our intuition.

The Trans-Personal

This is where we move gently from the realm of rational speculation, with ideas based within the framework of science, neuro-science, behaviourism and anthropology through the filters of personal psychology and into the mystical realms of the transpersonal.

Here we are in the shadowy areas of philosophy, metaphysics and belief and move far from the domain of empiricism and objectivity.

Personal experience is constructed (we spoke of radical constructivism earlier). It is constructed from elements of the 'world out there' as relayed by our senses and interpreted through the filters of our unconscious mind.

It was Jung who started to write specifically about his observations that there were certain ideas, images or archetypes which were common to all cultures. He coined the term 'the collective unconscious'.

In some cases it is the over simplification of his ideas which have led to confusion.

Theosophists under the tutelage of Madam Blavatsky were introduced to a world of 'Ascended Masters' and contact with 'Akashic Records'...

Edgar Cacy, the sleeping prophet, did more than his fair share in terms of the dissemination of the Atlantean Mythos (in terms of the lost spiritual paradise where every '*New Age spiritual teacher*' seems to have a link) as well as his connection to the 'library of the ages'; the Akasha.

To many Jung's 'collective unconscious' was the 'scientific' (or at least academic/psychological) validation of these ideas.

Of course Jung's own conversations with "daemons" and "spirit guides" seemed to cement the idea that 'at last' the sciences were agreeing with 'traditional teachings'.

I'm afraid I don't quite see it that way.

I am of course open to the idea that my interpretations are limited and a further misunderstanding of Jung's ideas – but I am willing to reconsider each of them in the light of new information.

So what was Jung actually saying?

Well it is my belief that Jung was talking about that part of our mind which has nothing to do with personal experience and everything to do with cultural stories, myths – shared ideas.

Jung wrote:

> "My thesis then, is as follows, in addition to our immediate consciousness, which of a thoroughly personal nature and which we believe to be the only empirical psyche there exists a second system of a collective, universal and impersonal nature which is identical in all individuals. This collective unconscious does not develop individually but is inherited. It consists of pre-existent forms, the archetypes, which can only become conscious secondarily and which give definite form to certain psychic contents."
>
> (Jung, 1996)
>
> (note Jung died in 1961, but his works have been reprinted, collected and collated ever since his death)

So we have some very specific words we need to look at the meaning of.

Some claim that *Monopsychism* was the idea that Jung was actually talking about; a mind to mind link with others across time.

Many New Age writers have jumped on this idea and proclaimed that Jung was 'brave enough' to present the idea that there is a kind of 'unconscious energy that lives forever'. (Healey, 2005)

For me this is one step too far, at the moment. Jung, I believe, was actually describing the pre-disposition of the mind to draw upon ideas and concepts (forms) that have developed as a result of humanity rather than outside of it. In the same way we could, in biology, talk about a 'collective leg' as a 'form', a notion, a shared idea.

There is something very Neo-Platonic and Aristotelian in this idea – the suggestion of 'original forms' and 'the essence of form'; but that is for another time and place.

So whereas the *collective consciousness* as proposed by earlier writers (Durkhiem, 1893), and the *consensus reality* I have been talking about, is all about personal and cultural interpretations of the sensory information; Jung's Collective Unconscious, is that part of our mind which is pre-disposed to create cultural 'forms', 'icons' and 'symbols'.

I maintain that it is to these symbols we assign mythic qualities, religious allegory and personal metaphor.

As 'new' ideas and images enter our consciousness there is the opportunity, through cultural evolution for these ideas to develop as cultural icons within the unconscious and over time become part of the 'collective unconscious'. If this is the case then the archetypes, symbols and images Jung refers to evolve in step with human development and therefore not (in all likelihood) transplanted into it by other non-corporeal (extraterrestrial) entities or civilizations.

Many New Age folk are worried by the word 'EGO' and maintain that they need to keep 'ego out of it' when it comes to spiritual matters.

I'm afraid I can't quite agree with their assertion, but have empathy with what I think they are implying.

Ego is, in many ways, simply the level at which we are consciously aware. It comes from the Latin word meaning 'I'.

In all regards the ego is how I define my-self; my self-esteem (although I dislike that phrase); the conscious thinking self.

Some spiritual traditions regard the ego in negative ways; we can be ego-led - we refer to someone who is self-absorbed as being an egotist.

The Ego is one dimension of the personality and true if it is the only dimension then perhaps the individual ceases to be able to function in all but the most needy and demanding of ways.

Of course ego cannot really exist in isolation for all human beings have a subconscious (unconscious) dimension to their personality.

Jung went onto suggest that the ego is at the core of our Persona – which is the 'mask' of self we present to the outside world. It is our 'social face'.

In a psychological sense the danger of one being defined simply by their 'persona' is not overly healthy. Such a connection will result in the individual being overly concerned with what people think about them rather than who they feel they 'are' or 'want' to be.

Jung was at pains to distance himself from certain of Freud's theories when it came to 'repression of the impulses' but was willing to recognize the importance of subconscious memories in the shaping of our personality.

These memories help shape and modify our perceptions and so influence our attitudes, values and behaviours.

Alongside these memories within the unconscious are what Jung referred to as 'denied psychic material'. This refers to the memories, associations that have either been dropped from conscious awareness or have not yet been made part of it.

The 'denied psychic material' and 'subconscious memories' form part of Jung called the Personal Unconscious.

The Collective Unconscious, as far as Jung was concerned, is the centre of all unconscious information which does not derive from personal experience. As mentioned earlier, its contents and images appear to be shared with people of different times and different cultures.

Jung maintained that just like the human body represented a 'whole museum' of organs, each with a long evolutionary period behind them, so to the mind is organized in a similar way.

Within the Collective Unconscious are Archetypes, images and ideas, which actually define a predisposition to respond to the world in different ways.

These archetypes include the anima (male) and animus (female); the shadow; the self amongst others which would are easily recognized within our cultural stories and myths – the magician, the syzygy (sacred twins), the wise man/woman, the mother and so on.

Jung and Psychic Energy...

Let's put the record straight here.

In 1928 Jung published an essay entitled "On Psychic Energy" which informs much of what we know today as psychodynamics.

We can appreciate the fact that physical energy allows the body to act upon the physical world, psychological (or psychic) energy acts upon the mental world – thoughts.

In a very real sense Jung's notion of psychic energy was distinct from, and possibly opposed to, the Eastern mystical notion of spiritual energy. Today many neurologists would accept that the 'energy' measured by brain imaging is a direct correlate to physical energy which powers the body.

Nowhere in this aspect of Jung's work do we find any basis for support in 'psychic energy' being responsible for the vast array of abilities claimed within the New Age literature.

Jung did, however, have 'spirit guides' one of whom was Philemon.

The Red Book, also known as Liber Nous, is a short book written by Jung between 1914 and 1930.

The 'relationship' with Philemon was described by Jung as a kind of experiment, a voluntary confrontation with the unconscious. (Jaffe, 1961).

He said that:-

> *The years when I pursued the inner images were the most important in my life. Everything else is to be derived from this.*

In a period of his life which some have said represented a 'mental breakdown' of some kind, Jung maintained that:-

> "Philemon and other figures of my fantasies brought home to me the crucial insight that there are things in the psyche which I do not produce, but which produce themselves and have their own life. Philemon represented a force that was not myself. In my fantasies I held conversations with him, and he said things which I had not consciously thought. […] Psychologically, Philemon represented superior insight."

Numerous Christian and some other orthodox religious writers maintain that Jung's 'dabbling' within the 'occult' has anti-Christian routes and that Philemon, and Jung's other 'spirit guides' were demons in disguise 'on a mission' to promote and make reasonable the 'Devils Work'.

So just has Jung has become the 'darling' of certain New Age thinkers, he has also been portrayed as a 'deluded sorcerer' peddling occult philosophies under the guise of science.

> We must evaluate Jung's psychology in the light of his heretical theology.
>
> After his break from discipleship with Freud, Jung let himself slip into an intense inner conflict—viewed by some as "a creative psychosis"—that shaped the lifelong development of his thinking. He saw it as a way to access what he believed was his "unconscious," but from the Biblical point of view, we can only describe it as an embrace of his sinful nature and the demonic realm.
>
> (Nathan, 2008)

In my opinion neither of these analyses is useful. Jung was, I believe, talking about a personal connection to areas of consciousness accessible through 'trance' or other altered states.

Whilst Jung himself maintained that the information from such 'guides' seemed to have a source which was beyond the self, perhaps the unconscious representations (the personality and form of Philemon if you like) were constructed from cultural themes and archetypes existing within what he would call the collective unconscious.

Jung wrote that when we cease to manage these representations we are, in effect, possessed.

He wrote that:-

"Possession, though old-fashioned, has by no means become obsolete; only the name has changed. Formerly they spoke of 'evil spirits,' now we call them 'neurosis' or 'unconscious complexes.'"

And that:-

"Possession is a primordial psychic phenomenon" that *"denotes a peculiar state of mind characterized by the fact that certain psychic contents, the so-called complexes, take over the control of the total personality in place of the ego, at least temporarily, to such a degree that the free will of the ego is suspended."*

So in a very real sense when we are unaware of the conflicts within our unconscious mind they may manifest as controlling 'entities' (given form by cultural images and archetypes) so creating breakdown of the psyche; loss of personal identity and atypical behavioural responses.

THE COSMOS

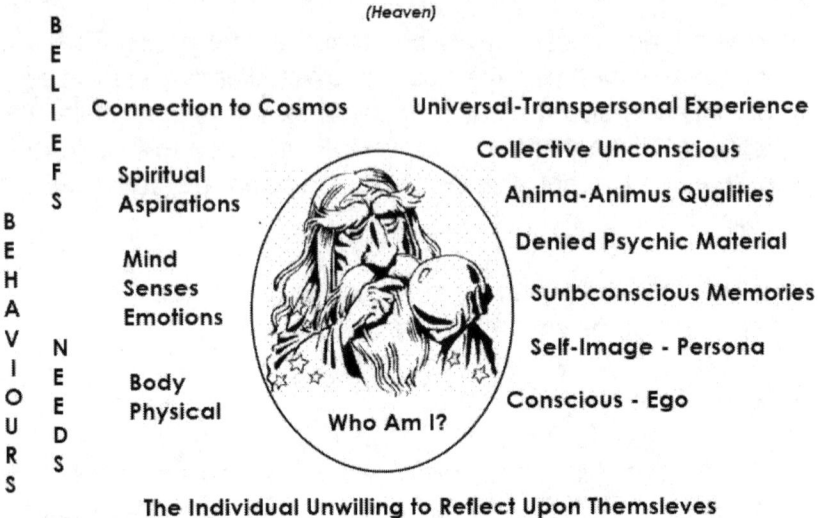

The Cosmos Seeking To Understand Itself
(Heaven)

BELIEFS

BEHAVIOURS

NEEDS

Connection to Cosmos

Spiritual Aspirations

Mind
Senses
Emotions

Body
Physical

Universal-Transpersonal Experience

Collective Unconscious

Anima-Animus Qualities

Denied Psychic Material

Sunbconscious Memories

Self-Image - Persona

Conscious - Ego

Who Am I?

The Individual Unwilling to Reflect Upon Themsleves
(Hell)

An insight into how individuals express their experience of each of these 'levels of awareness' allows for an understanding of how their present-self links with an idealized, spiritual, concept of self.

An interesting thought here, which will be immediately dismissed by some, is that the 'spiritual beings' we sense, if indeed we do, are projections of our ego and/or psyche onto the source of the information we sense as being 'transpersonal' (beyond the self).

The reason, perhaps, some will find this uncomfortable is that they have a belief system (or need) which requires the survival of the personality and the sense that there must be somewhere better; that there is a master plan or some kind of order in the Cosmos which brings comfort when life (on Earth) is so difficult.

28088640484

Levels of Communication

Inter-Personal

Communication between two or more individuals

A mixture of verbal and non-verbal techniques

The focus is to share ideas, opinions, thoughts and feelings

Based within the rational, observable and personal

Intra-Personal

Self-Talk or Internal Dialogue

Thoughts, Thinking, Meta-Cognition, Conscience

The focus is generally about personal responses to 'the world'

A mixture of rational and symbolic language

Trans-Personal

Thoughts, Ideas or Insights gained through spiritual means

Meditation, Contemplation, Prayer, Reflection

The focus is to seek deeper understanding; search for meaning

Probably best considered as symbolic and metaphorical

Psychic

Sharing of transpersonal insights with others

Exploring deeper meaning within inter and intra personal relationships

One of my problems with some 'psychics', 'mediums' and 'clairvoyants' is their apparent claim that they '**know**' what is best for others and that they can guide or advise – or more generally 'tell' their clients things and 'give them information'.

The danger is that this information and knowledge is given authority because it doesn't come from 'Psychic Phil', 'Spiritualist Stacy' or 'Medium Martha' but from 'their' unique contact with the 'spiritual realms'.

Now, perhaps this is really what is happening, but what if it's not?

It may be that:-

Phil, Stacy and Martha are simply be offering their wisdom, experience, knowledge and intuitions – which could be very insightful, valuable and transformational

It may be that:-

Phil, Stacy and Martha are abdicating personal responsibility for the advice, opinions and ideas they give since 'it didn't come from them, but through them'.

But are:-

Phil, Stacy and Martha failing to honour and recognize their own power and personal relationship with the Cosmos?

And are:-

Phil, Stacy and Martha are simply in it for the kudos, marketing and money?

Now I am **not** for one minute suggesting that all clairvoyants, mediums, psychics are being fraudulent. I am suggesting that it is worth considering the claims that are being made and the evidence which is being presented in the context of the belief system, experience and philosophical stance of the individual.

I maintain that those 'readers' who are effective in their work, whether they are claiming psychic, mediumistic or other 'powers', are actively engaging people in a consideration of their journey, their choices and their abilities. (I write more about this in my book Transformational Readings).

Also, if you recall, my basic argument is that we are all psychic and can learn to be open to others by engaging our senses in the various ways already described.

By paying attention to what someone says, how they say it and what their body language implies you are communicating in emotional, physical and intellectual ways.

When you stop and apply the same sensory focus on yourself you may be able to open yourself to intuition as well as transpersonal awareness and insights.

For example I may look at a doodle someone has drawn, or a Tarot card they have selected and find ways of commenting upon what I 'sense' that specific image means to them; how they relate to it and the questions I feel would be useful for them to consider.

This is part of my total sensory (psychic) approach BUT I may also catch a 'glimpse' of an 'idea', 'moment' or 'phrase' which comes from something beyond 'me'. Some may want to ascribe this information to 'spirit' and in a sense I guess it is. For me it is part of the Cosmos to which I am now being open and so translate ideas, feelings and symbols into words, associations and meaning.

These transpersonal ideas, feelings and symbols (which are abstract) are given physicality as my consciousness transcribes and codes the experience.

In brief then, when I relay that insight, as in when I commuunicate generally, I am offering something that is at least two steps removed from the original, personal experience. Of course YOU, by simply processing what I have offered, dilute the message even further.

In such cases the only authority that insight can have is based upon the relevance it has as a question to the person being offered it.

And here, for me, is an important point.

If I make a statement based upon my intuition, psychic or mediumistic connection then it is being heard as a pronouncement and does not generally engage the listener in their own thinking.

If I use the same intuition and phrase it as a question the listener is being invited to consider a possibility and a conversation might follow.

So you still want to develop your psychic abilities?

Get yourself a personal journal and keep daily records of your progress, ideas, thoughts, revelations, challenges...

Use it as a tool for growth and reflection.

Sorted, OK, so here's a seven step plan which, if you follow carefully and with thought will allow you to develop total sensory perception.

I will assume that you have considered carefully the information about the psychology of human communication.

To reiterate:-

Words mean what we agree they mean.

You create personal realities based upon your perceptions.

Your perceptions are influenced by your unconscious mind, in that 'it' will influence the way you interpret your sensory input.

You create meaning and understanding from what you interpret.

When you share your experience you are sharing something which has been processed within your mind and not the original experience.

When you hear another person's experience you turn that into something you can make sense of and understand. You create your version of their experience.

Each of us has a repertoire of non-verbal communication patterns which, for the most part, are processed unconsciously by other people so giving them a 'sense' about what we are saying, how we are saying it and how thus defining a personal reaction which may not be directly understood by the conscious mind.

785381990

Our unconscious mind directs our conscious attention in subtle ways. This direction of attention relates directly to our expectations, our beliefs, our previous experience, our associations and the situation we find ourselves in.

Ideas and thoughts 'pop into' consciousness from our unconscious mind. They can be the result of our unconscious having concluded some sort of processing; an intuition or idea which relates to our experiences and reactions to similar past experiences; from some other (apparently) trans-personal source which may be projections onto (or from) the collective unconscious; from some *denied psychic material* or from a sense of connection to the cosmos.

Personal *intuition* is a mixture of personal experiences, past associations, rapid cognition, links with the collective unconscious and the imagery therein and possible links with altered states of consciousness and its specific iconography. All of which has the feel of a 'knowing' that originates from beyond the self.

Got it?

Well if so let us begin...

The seven steps I am proposing for psychic (total sensory) perception are as follows

1. Clarity
2. Focus
3. Presence
4. Congruence
5. Intention
6. Ownership
7. Feedback

Over the next few pages we will explore each in a little more detail and suggest exercises which may help you explore some of the ideas. I suggest you obtain a note book in which to record your responses to each of the ideas and your reactions to them.

The exercises are meant to be completed in order and there is no need to rush.

Take about a week for each of the seven steps.

Week One Focus : Clarity

Clarity is your ability to put some of yourself aside so that you can be open to the your external, internal and transpersonal world AND know when you are shifting between them.

In essence we could describe this as clairvoyance.

Activity 1

Make a list of the things you believe about people, the way the world works and spiritual issues.

Let's start with People

Answer these questions carefully and honestly.

Do you believe, really believe that all people are inherently 'good at heart' or do you believe that there are some 'really evil' people in the world?

How would you recognize a 'good person'?

How would you recognize an 'evil person'?

What turn's you off people?

What qualities in another person attract you?

Exploration

These are important questions. Your answers will allow you to explore not only the values which underpin your beliefs, but also your expectations.

How would you recognize a 'good person'?

How would you recognize an 'evil person'?

Once you can describe how you would recognize a good or evil person you can reflect upon the expectations you have on others; the possible prejudices you have when meeting people who have a different cultural or personal value system.

Have you defined certain 'behaviours' as being good or certain 'values and attitudes' – can you distinguish between them?

Have you now fallen into the 'trap' of believing that you never *judge a book by its cover* or *never define the person by their behaviour?*

These are wonderful pieces of rhetoric but are you saying them because you 'know' that snap judgments about people is something your cultural or spiritual tradition sees as being a 'bad' thing.

Remember we are making judgments about people and situations all of the time – it's a survival thing – the real question is at what point do your judgments stop you from engaging on a deeper level with the people you meet.

What turn's you off people?

This question, when answered honestly, again gives you insight into your values, attitudes and expectations.

What attracts you to another person?

These are the qualities which you will value in others; the ones which will actually shape your judgment of them.

The things which 'turn you off' a person and a thing which 'attracts you to a person' will have clear polarities. For example if good grooming attracts you then someone who does not take any pride in their appearance may well 'turn you off'.

So for each of these 'turn on' – 'turn off' qualities create a list as follows

Likes	**Dislikes**
Good Grooming	No interest in appearance
Smile	Always frowning
Smiling Eyes	
	Shabby clothes

Ok, I think you get the idea.

If you have listed a dislike which is not the polarity of a like, then make sure you think about what the opposite is and write into the list.

If you have listed a like which does not have its opposite in your dislike column then add it to the list; the idea is to create a 'balanced' list of likes and dislikes.

So were you able to come up with the things you liked in another person more easily than the things you disliked. In short are you more aware of the things you like or dislike in others?

What happens if you now rewrite the entire list in order of priority?

For example starting with the most 'liked' quality?

Were you able to find the 'opposite' quality for every like/dislike and when you did do you think they have the same 'weight'.

For example you may strongly dislike 'bad grooming' BUT good grooming is not high on your list of priorities.

This exercise is, of course, about you and your perceptions. In order to see other clearly you need to be aware of the judgments you make about them. The more honest you are about what see and respond to the more honest you can be about what can be 'blind' to.

Activity 2

The way the world/cosmos works.

Here are some statements, give each a score out of ten for how much you agree with them. A score of ten means that totally, whole-heartedly agree whereas a score of zero means you totally disagree.

Statement	Score
Shit Happens	
Everything works out for the best eventually	
God (The Cosmos) has a plan	
The world is neither totally good nor totally evil	
If I take an active role in my life then things will work out	
Human beings are at best a virus making the Earth ill	
What I do has no effect on the Cosmos in any meaningful way	
Every challenge, every problem is a blessing and a lesson in disguise	
If I live in harmony with the Earth then the Earth will provide	
People are simply one step in a continuing evolutionary process	
The material world is an illusion we create	
My life in the here and now is the result of Karma	
We create our own realities	
The World, the Cosmos, has no opinion about me or anyone else	
The more I learn about the world the less I know about me	
The more I know about me the more I connect with the world	
In the long term it doesn't matter what I do, life creates problems	
From a whole world perspective there's no such thing as choice	
There is no such thing as free-will	
Events which happen elsewhere are no concern of mine	
If I can't change it why would I worry about it?	
Life is what you make it not what it makes of you	

Exploration

Looking carefully at your answers will help you reflect upon those things which underpin your personal values and attitudes. They hint at your (possibly) unconscious belief systems.

If you list the statements in order of acceptance you may find some interesting patterns emerging. Which statements hint at a fatalistic view of your universe; which are optimistic, which pessimistic, which hopeful?

From a review of these statements are you someone who seems to have a faith some kind of 'intention' or 'design'. More importantly you may gain an insight into how you interact with your concept of the universe.

An interesting question here is the degree to which you feel you have free-will, the ability to change your personal path and/or the degree of predetermination you feel your life is subject to.

Underpinning Values

Activity 3

Below you'll find a list of words. As you read each think about the feelings you have about them and what they evoke for you.

Make a note of your thoughts, feelings and responses to each word or phrase.

Word	Your feelings, reactions, thoughts
GHOST	
SPIRIT	
GOD	
CHURCH	
PAGAN	
QUIJA BOARD	
FORTUNE TELLING	
ASTROLOGY	
MAGIC	
WITCH	
TAROT CARDS	
HOLY SPIRIT	
SOUL	
SCIENCE	
MEDICINE	
HEALING	
PRAYER	
SPELL	
CURSE	
VOODOO	
CATHOLIC	
GNOSTIC	
AGNOSTIC	
ATHEIST	
ISLAM	
CHRISTIAN	
JESUS	
BUDDHA	
LAO TSE	
OCCULT	
MASONIC	
SEX	
KARMA	

Exploration

Many of the words above have strong, emotional triggers. There will be positive associations and possibly negative associations.

Look at the list and what you wrote next to each word or short phrase. What was your immediate, gut reaction to words like Occult, Witch, Quija?

What about your reaction to the word God, Church or Pagan?

Your immediate, gut-level, reactions will be based upon your prejudices.

Here are some useful questions to drive your self-exploration.

a) What do you REALLY know about the words you had a negative reaction to?

b) What beliefs, values or attitudes are suggested to you by the words you had a strong reaction to?

c) Where do your opinions come from in relation to the words you have a strong emotional reaction to?

Real prejudice thrives when there is an abundance of opinion and a lack of knowledge or direct, meaningful, experience.

Those with a strong Christian ethic may have certain reservations about words like Occult, Quija, Witch, Pagan and so on.

But where do these personal reactions come from?

Is it simply about religious doctrine, opinion and statements of faith?

Apart from religious teachings which suggest you avoid people who 'dabble in the Occult' what information do you actually have about occultists?

Are your personal values, beliefs and attitudes closing you down to the truths and experiences of others?

To be truly open to another's world view you have to be able to ask questions based upon the desire to find out, rather than the desire to challenge. Listening to someone else's spiritual or religious opinion does not mean you become infected with their ideas as some of the more fundamental groups will maintain, it does mean that you are willing to explore them and their world.

I maintain that the more insecure one is about their opinion, faith or belief the less they are able to tolerate the ideas and experience of others. Certainly there are evangelical types that I have met who close-down any potentially controversial discussion because they claim to 'know' that theirs is the 'truth' and by extension everything else must be wrong.

If a personal world is so closed to the ideas of others then there is NO possibility of developing a meaningful connection of any kind, let alone a psychic one.

So, in order to develop your own sensory/psychic perception you need to find ways to challenge your own prejudice and become open to (not victim of) the worlds of others.

Reflecting on the ideas raised in the last three activities is a starting point. All personal and psychic development begins with you. Understanding some of your unconscious prejudices and triggers is the first step in being able to give your attention in such a way as to be truly insightful.

Week Two Focus : FOCUS

I have a simple phrase which I think explains why focus is an important step in psychic and personal development.

Attention Goes Where Emotion Flows

So if you have really thought about the issues coming from last week's activities then you will realize that the emotional hooks you have been exploring actually 'get in the way' of giving attention to another person, place or situation.

Your ability to 'recognise' and 'read' the body language clues mentioned earlier in this book rely on you being able to give your undivided attention to another person – without you needing to bring the focus back to you.

Here are some questions for you to consider...

How soon after the start of the conversation do you ask questions about the other person's wellbeing?

When you ask such questions do you really listen and reflect upon what they tell you OR do you use their answers as a segue into YOUR stuff?

When asked 'How are things?' do you unload your stuff without pause or consideration for the listener?

How much of any conversation is about YOU?

Do you 'stomp all over' the other persons comments or questions with your own free-flowing monologue?

Do you really CARE about the people you are in conversation with?

Do you walk into a room an open your mouth with paying any attention to what the person in that room is currently doing or saying?

You cannot notice anyone or anything else when you are so focused on yourself. This, I maintain, is the 'ego' which many spiritual folks mean when they suggest that 'ego get's in the way'.

Since your ego is you (thinking bank to Jung's ideas above) then you need to be self-aware enough to know when and how to get out of your own way.

There's a time and a place for you to share your experience, knowledge and opinion but this is rarely when you are listening to someone else, or entering into a new environment (place/space)

This week's exercises then are about learning that you can choose where to place your attention in everyday situations and so notice more about less.

Activity 1

Close your eyes and create a memory, picture or sense of a room in your house you **were** in an hour or so ago.

Now focus your mind on one surface in that room which you know had, or should have some items on it. For example if you were thinking of your bedroom, perhaps you could picture your dressing table; or if it was the bathroom perhaps you could picture the bathroom cabinet.

OK

Now compile a list of things that you KNOW are on that surface.

Describe each item in detail – the brand name, the colour, the shape, what it is made of, what it contains, is it full – empty or half empty, is there a price tag still on it – get the idea?

When you've completed this list think of another location and do the same again.

When you've described three locations take the time to check how accurate your observations were.

Exploration

Some of you will have retained a good deal of information; some of you may not.

Remember you can only remember the things you pay attention to.

So how good was your recall?

Or, in other words, how much attention you pay to things around you?

Think back to how you were recalling the various places in the activity above.

What was your strongest sense...

SEEING – were you able to see in colour as if you were looking at a picture; did you have a sense of 'being there' – as in looking through your own eyes rather than seeing a photograph?

HEARING – were you able to 'hear' sounds related to the places you were imagining?

FEELING – could you feel textures, or get the sense that you could've reached out and 'felt' the surfaces you were concentrating on?

THINKING – did you have a sense of recalling what was there rather than creating (re-creating) an picture; were you telling yourself what was there (as in self-talking)?

SMELLING – were you able to physically access a sense of smell or some kind of odour associated with the situation you were picturing; could you recreate or imagine a smell?

You may have had an equally strong 'sense' from all of these sensory modalities, generally however, you may feel that one or two are more strongly developed than the others.

Activity 2

Whilst you are out and about interacting with the world, focus on one particular sense a day. Now of course you will need to pay attention to all sensory information as you are interacting with the material world BUT on each day re-focus and concentrate on ONE aspect of your sensory world in the following order:-

Day 1

Pay particular attention to what you SEE. Notice colours, shapes, patterns, hues, details. Try to imagine seeing the objects you encounter from a different perspective – above, below, left, right, reversed, in different colours.

The idea is to practice and develop your visual acuity and your visual imagination.

Day 2

Pay particular attention to your sound-scape – what you HEAR. Notice the tones, the frequencies, the pitch, the tempo. Try to imagine hearing the sounds in our environment and the sound patterns (vocalizations) of the people you are communicating with. Try to re-hear the sounds and change the tone, tempo, timbre, volume and spatial elements (where you think the sounds are coming from).

The idea is to practice and develop your aural acuity and aural imagination.

Day 3

Pay particular attention to the textures of things within your environment. Notice how smooth, sharp, rough, rounded, slick things are. Try to imagine touching a thing and how it feels BEFORE you touch it. Notice the difference between expectation and reality.

The idea is to practice and develop your tactile sense and your ability to imagine touch, feel.

Day 4

Pay particular attention to how you fee – your emotions. What things in your environment generate a feeling, emotion, sensitivity within you?

Notice how you emotionally react to people, place, situation and explore the source of those feelings. (Look back at previous activities where you have considered your emotional hooks and 'prejudices').

Imagine a situation that you will know you will find yourself in. and record your anticipated emotions and feelings. Then take note of the similarities and differences between anticipated and actual emotions that were triggered for each situation.

Start to compile a list of words which describe your emotions. Apparently there are 3,000 words which describe emotion in the English language. (Elert, 2013) How many do you use, know or have felt?

The idea is to develop and extend your emotional awareness and personal, emotional intelligence/literacy.

Day 5

As you experience your day, all aspects of your day, create and maintain an 'internal commentary' of what you are doing, thinking, seeing, feeling, touching.

This will not be that easy to maintain since it will split your conscious attention between your outer world and your inner world. But the idea is to be the narrator of your own experience.

At the end of the day choose one or two experiences from that day and close your eyes re-tell or re-describe the incident in as much detail as possible.

The idea behind this exercise is to allow you to develop and extend your ability to 'step back' from the immediate, personal experience and reflect from a neutral, commentators point of view.

Day 6

This may well be the most challenging exercise in this series. Your focus will be on the quality of your inter-personal communication skills.

It may be that you will want to spread this particular activity across several days. Completion of the task is not about finishing the tasks quickly, but in exploring each for your own interest and development.

During as many conversations as possible during the day engage in each of the following:-

   a) Match the breathing of the person you are speaking to

   b) Pause for at least three breaths before answering any question they ask or before you offer an opinion

   c) Create space for the person you are conversing with to extend their comments, idea, thoughts

   d) Avoid using the word BUT – as in "Yes but..." – instead try to use AND, EVEN THOUGH, WHAT ABOUT instead

   e) Avoid using the word WHY – as in requesting an explanation – instead try using WHAT, HOW, WHO, WHEN, WHERE

   f) Avoid using the words MUST, SHOULD and OUGHT – instead try to use the words POSSIBLY, MAY, COULD, MIGHT

Day 7

This is your 'people watching day'.

Try to find a block of time when you can sit and watch the interactions of others. Notice their body language, the inter-play of words and gestures. You don't have to be close enough to hear what is being said, nor do you have to behave like some stalker, private eye or weird voyeur. You simply sit back and watch the world go by.

After a while you will notice patterns of behaviour (non-verbal communication) and possibly have an insight into what you think might be the relationship between the people you are watching.

This is where all that stuff about body language and if you are close enough, micro-expressions and eye movement comes into play.

Try to create a story about the people you are watching.

- Who are they?
- What is their relationship?
- How much do they like or listen to each other?
- What kind of work do they do?
- Where have they just come from?
- Where are they going next?
- Who is leading the conversation and what is their agenda?
- Are they flirting?
- Is this a business meeting?
- Is one or the other sending out 'mixed messages'
- What will these people be doing in three hours time?

Whether you are right or wrong about your assumptions does not matter. What does matter is that you are looking, thinking and using deduction reasoning and your imagination to link the patterns of behaviour you are observing to a **possible** life story.

Lovers of the Sherlock Holmes stories will be aware that this is the kind of information being used by the master sleuth to make mysterious summations as to a clients (or suspects) where-a-bouts, motives, actions and agendas.

In every sense of the word this is **real psychic development** since you are using the mind, the information from your senses and your intuition (as defined above) to create possible realities and meaningful stories. It is the kind of process you do every day unconsciously.

Exploration

The first five exercises are all about developing your sensory acuity and in doing so noticing the richness of experience which generally bypasses your conscious mind and is processed by your unconscious. Rather than being vaguely aware of your surroundings and the people in it you are attempting to become very aware of the subtleties of the world you walk through every day.

The exercise for day six is particularly challenging and is all about trying to explore the blocks and avenues to effective interpersonal communication.

Psychologically we know there are certain things which encourage rapport between people and things which destroy rapport.

When people are en rapport their breathing patterns and body language tend to sync. Body postures will tend towards mirroring each other and breathing rates and positions my also sync.

If trying to match these things consciously there is a danger of appearing to mimic rather than developing rapport. Your behaviour, as the person seeking to develop rapport, needs to be as subtle and understated as possible.

The whole point of giving a breath or two before adding your two-penny worth into a conversation is twofold:-

a) You demonstrate that you have listened to and are considering what has just been said

b) You give yourself time to phrase a response so you don't have to worry about doing so whilst the other person is speaking; so, in effect, not listening.

Developing Sensory Acuity

This kind of active listening means that you need to free yourself from your immediate agenda and so focusing on what has and is being said.

You have two ears and one mouth and listening requires you to maintain the same relative proportions (at least) between speaking and listening.

In terms of language...

WHY questions are really about justification of particular idea or behaviour (Why did you do that? : Why do you feel that way) and as such have their place. However if you use WHAT, HOW, WHEN, WHO, WHERE instead in a question you may find you get some different and more informative responses.

For example:-

"I'm so angry at Bob"

The why question, which let's face it is probably what the speaker is expecting since it gives them permission to tell you all about Bob, is about justifying the feeling of anger.

If you were to ask...

"So what was it that causes you to feel this anger?"

You may find that the quality of reflection from the speaker is increased. From a therapeutic point of view a great deal of personal change work can be accomplished by simply asking 'what specifically'; 'when specifically" ; 'how specifically' ; 'where specifically' ; 'who specifically' ...

One VITAL caveat...

Never ask a question unless you know what you can do with the answer. This level of questioning by-passes some of the normal, anticipated inter-personal communication channels and asks the speaker to think about how they relate to what they are saying.

So what about BUT?

Well there are so many times when the 'Yes But' response is used without really thinking about what is possibly being unconsciously stated or indeed understood.

For example..

"I think that Bob's solution is the best one..."

"Yes so do I .... BUT..."

This immediately creates a sense that you agree but don't agree; that you understand but don't understand.

The BUT word often negates the sentiment of what was said before...

I agree with you ... BUT ...

Notice that the word AND implies an equality between the phrase before it and the phrase which follows...

"I agree AND what about... ?'

The same is true of the phrase 'even though'...

Now I'm not expecting you to immediately see how relevant this kind of linguistic game playing can be, but if you monitor your own reactions to the 'Yes But-ers' ; "Event Thougher's" ; and Yes And-ers' you will notice the differences in emotional tension.

You will immediately recognize the differences between these two statements..

"You should know better..."

The Yes But Syndrome

"I would have thought you might have known better..."

Both say the same thing, but one has an edge, a sense of a command, the other has a sense of disappointment.

In NLP these words are called 'modal operators of necessity' (Must, Should, Ought) and 'modal operators of possibility' (May, Could, Might).

Using a word from the 'necessity' list immediately implies and order, a command or a rebuke.

Using a word from the 'possibility' list opens up a conversation which focuses on alternative behaviours, attitudes, thinking and values.

The Sherlock Holmes activity (day seven) is really about making you conscious of those guesses, assumptions and conclusions your unconscious mind is already really good at making. The only difference is that when you unconsciously process this information the results are presented to your conscious mind as a 'sense', a 'feeling', an 'intuition'.

This exercise is about the ideas expressed by Malcolm Gladwell (Blink), Jung (Collective Unconscious) and what I have defined as intuition earlier in this book.

By becoming conscious of these processes and through an understanding of what may be going on in the mind you are able to 'tweek' the unconscious processes, so developing them in the light of conscious feedback.

Week Three Focus : Presence

In many ways we all spend far too much time 'BECOMING' rather than 'BEING'.

Over the last couple of weeks you will have noticed your sensory acuity developing; your ability to notice things increasing and the quality of your inter-personal communication. Now the challenge is to remain 'present' in whatever you are doing whenever you are doing it – perhaps I should say having the choice to remain present.

Our minds are always active, always connecting, always busy. Learning to still it in order to be 'present' is the challenge of this week and it will start with 'meditation'.

Now here's the thing there are as many pieces of advice about meditation as there are people doing meditation. So let's stop and think about what I mean by meditation.

First of all **'it's not'** about making your mind blank. As Wikipedia says...

> *The term meditation refers to a broad variety of practices (much like the term sports) that includes techniques designed to promote relaxation, build internal energy or life force and develop compassion, love, patience, generosity and forgiveness.*
>
> *A particularly ambitious form of meditation aims at effortlessly sustained single-pointed concentration single-pointed analysis, meant to enable its practitioner to enjoy a sense of well-being while engaging in any life activity.*
>
> (Wikipedia)

Meditation has some very interesting health benefits (Mayho, 1998) but the kind of meditation we're going to be looking at here is often called 'mindfulness' meditation.

In the Buddhist Tradition 'Mindfulness Meditation' is described as:-

> *In mindfulness, or shamatha, meditation, we are trying to achieve a mind that is stable and calm. What we begin to discover is that this calmness or harmony is a natural aspect of the mind. Through mindfulness practice we are just developing and strengthening it, and eventually we are able to remain peacefully in our mind without struggling. Our mind naturally feels content.*
>
> *An important point is that when we are in a mindful state, there is still intelligence. It's not as if we blank out. Sometimes people think that a person who is in deep meditation doesn't know what's going on—that it's like being asleep. In fact, there are meditative states where you deny sense perceptions their function, but this is not the accomplishment of shamatha practice.*
>
> (Rinpoche, 2008)

There are three basic aspects in this meditation technique: body, breath and thoughts.

Body

You need to find a space where you can sit, comfortably, with no added stress or tension being placed on any part of the body.

Perform a 'body scan' and notice where you are holding tension. One way to help reduce muscle tension is to tense muscles in turn and then consciously let them relax. Feel the difference, and take some time to allow each muscle relax.

Notice where the 'centre' of your body is... well do you feel your strength comes from. This could be interpreted as your bodies centre of gravity, but may feel like something different to you.

Be aware of the sounds of your body; your heartbeat – soon you will notice your breathing.

Breathing

Notice the rate, pace and position of your breathing. Feel your body react to each breath, the rise and fall of your chest, your diaphragm, the filling and emptying of your lungs.

If you want change your breathing pattern; perhaps in through the nose and out through the mouth; perhaps breathing in – holding for the count of two and breathing out for the count of three.

Notice how each breath effects your body, your awareness, your feelings, your sense of alertness.

Slower breathing may equate for you with feeling more relaxed or more awake.

As you breathe in, tense any muscles that still feel tense and then, on the out breath, allow that tension to relax.

Notice how your posture and breathing are linked...

Find the posture and breathing style/rate/position which allows you to focus on the now.

And then become aware of your thoughts...

Thoughts

Notice how your thoughts are chopping and changing direction; how your awareness is shifting moment to moment.

Rather than trying to limit your thinking, just follow the rambling flow of ideas. Notice that they can flow like a river; follow that river see where each though takes you.

Becoming aware of your thoughts and how they can be influenced by your breathing, your posture and your environment.

Watch every thought come and go, whether it be a worry, fear, anxiety or hope. When thoughts come up in your mind, don't ignore or suppress them but simply note them, remain calm and use your breathing as an anchor.

If you find yourself getting carried away in your thoughts, observe where your mind went off to, without judging, and simply return to your breathing. Remember not to be hard on yourself if this happens.

Coming back to the 'here and now'

Become aware of your feet, then a specific sound outside of yourself – perhaps in the room, building or street outside.

Sit for a minute or two, becoming aware of where you are.

Get up gradually.

There's a real link between breathing, physiology (posture), internal state and performance.

These exercises are about finding that link.

Try to find ten to fifteen minutes each day to practice this mindfulness technique.

As you develop a better sense of how this works for you, try to put it into practice in your daily routines. When walking notice your breathing, how your muscles tense and relax as you walk. Notice the way your body interacts with the world around it; how each foot fall contains information about the surface you are walking on.

Mindfulness meditation is not simply about sitting still and being quiet, sure that is part of the practice, but being mindful and present in the 'now' is the ultimate aim.

And YES, you have been developing mindfulness over the previous two weeks of suggested activity. *Clarity* and *Focus* are mindful activities.

You will see, I hope, that actively checking your current state is an essential component of preparing yourself for any formal meeting or engagement. A growing number of therapists are developing mindfulness practices for themselves prior to seeing clients as it helps them let-go of stuff from the last session and so being 'clear' for the next person they are going to see.

In terms of therapy, encouraging clients to develop mindfulness is proving to be of great value.

Let's face it when was the last time you did nothing... no TV, no InterNet, no 'phone, no interruptions...

We are constantly reacting or preparing to be proactive based upon what we are projecting into our future. So doing no-thing for a few minutes is quite refreshing.

In New Code NLP, John Grinder talks about the power of taking a *no-mind state* to a *problem state* and allowing internal, unconscious changes to happen. In my therapy work I have seen how powerful this can be.

During this week's mindfulness exercises ensure you spend a few minutes making a note of your experiences in your journal. In fact make one of your mindfulness sessions about writing in your journal.

Write a word, any word, and then keep adding ideas, thoughts and associations. This is called *'automatic writing'* or *'free association'* depending upon the particular school of thought you follow.

Notice the movement of your hand across the paper; the muscles which tense and relax in order to allow you to write; the free flow of words and associations; the links you make when you make them and how you reflect upon the stream of consciousness when you re-read what you have written later.

Be-ing in the moment means that you are open to whatever the moment brings, however it brings it and how you respond – body, breathing, mind (which includes thoughts, feelings, intuitions).

Week Four Focus : Congruence

Congruence is all about walking your talk; being your own behavioural model.

When your values, attitudes, beliefs are 'in line' with what you say and what you do then there is congruence.

The challenge is, then, you have to have a sense of what your values, attitudes and beliefs are. (Remember the first week of activities?).

So, assuming you are self-aware enough to be aware of these things how can you develop an understanding of when you are or are not being congruent?

Well one way is to become aware of 'perceptual positions'.

Most of the time we are in 'first position' - behaving from and within our own personal frame of reference.

We see things from our point of view; we respond with the words we choose based upon the way our unconscious mind presents the world to us.

It has to be this way if we are being 'real'.

But, it is possible to look at any situation from 'second position'. That is from the position or perspective of someone 'outside of yourself'.

Now let's be 'real' here. When we try to imagine how someone else is seeing a situation we are really engaging our imaginations; projecting our behaviours and assumptions upon them. BUT this does not invalidate the experience or what we can learn from it.

If you were to consider any recent conversation with another person you are recalling it from your perspective. You can choose to try and see it through 'their eyes' and so understand their reactions to you.

There is a "third perceptual position" and this is that of a neutral observer watching the drama un-fold; if you like the audience to a stage play.

The key difference between 'third position' and 'the other two', is that it can be emotionally neutral.

The following story is taken from my book (Jones, Ramblings of a Rational Mystic, 2011)

Today, a market, a cafe...

An old lady sits with her partner settling to enjoy a cup of tea and a slice of cake. Her shaky hand drops the cup of hot coffee; it splashes over her leg and onto the floor of the crowded stall. She grimaces as the hot liquid soaks through the material of her trousers.

The response of the 'caring humans' around her...

Partner ... "You stupid bitch look what you've done..."

The nearby tables - one group laughs, another group tuts and moves their seats away from the spreading puddle...

The cafe owner - rushes out, mop in hand...

The lady's partner shoves her aside, against the wall as he tries to rescue his egg and cress sandwich - the chairs scatter at the strength of his push.

She, still smarting from the scald, now red with embarrassment...

A helpless look in her eyes, her shoulders down - the body language of defeat...

Now the floor is cleaned, the tables are reset and she sits.

It is obvious that the cake has no further appeal; her embarrassment has taken the edge of her hunger.

Silently, inwardly reflective and possibly cursing herself...

Her partner looks at her, 'tuts', then gestures with a thumb "go get yourself another one..."

It's an order not a suggestion - she refuses; sitting quietly amid the anger, the looks, the comments and the sighs.

Slowly her hand moves to lift the damp material from her leg - it is a quiet, steady motion she does not want others to see.

She grimaces, her pain is silent, her humiliation complete.

During the whole incident only one person looked across the cafe and asked if she was OK, if she needed help...

The potential support of a stranger declined from a distance... a human contact lost amid the inhumane treatment she was the victim of.

Here is another Askew-like case. Oh not as extreme perhaps, but then each of the incidents that led to David Askews' death was in and of itself small, trivial and unremarkable.

One wonders what reality the 'cafe-lady' is returning to; how her day will develop and how she will find some kind of comfort, support and compassion. Her partner will certainly be huffing and puffing for most of the day; being aware of the next possible incident which will cause him embarrassment.

Sometimes I despair of the isolation that is a consequence of living within a community.

As you read the above piece notice YOUR reactions to the scene (this is the first person stuff); try to imagine the reactions, emotions of the author, the 'café-lady' and other onlookers (this would be second position) and then consider the whole scene from the point of view of an emotionally neutral commentator of the event who sees everyone and everything in it (this is third position).

The exercises this week are all about encouraging to shift perspective easily and fully associate with that perspective.

How do you do that?

Well first you have to notice the differences in your breathing, physiology, thinking and emotional state when you are firmly IN each of these perceptual positions.

What changes for you as you move from first to second and back...

Then from first to third and back...

Finally from second to third and back...

These internal changes may be small so pay attention to how you breathe, feel and think in each.

I know some people who notice that when they look at a memory, for example, their internal pictures change in quality as they move from perceptual position to perceptual position.

So that when they are in first position they seem to be looking through their own eyes; the picture is bright and colourful and panoramic. In second position it is like they are looking at a picture and see themselves in it and in third position the picture is like a series of large 'freeze frames' and are slightly duller in colour.

Now this was their experience.

What is yours?

In NLP we talk about modalities (which are see, hear, feel, think) and sub-modalities, the qualities of each of the modalities (bright, loud, colourful, sharp, distinct, stereo – and so on).

So here's the challenge. Think about a memory or situation. Explore differences in 'modalities' and 'submodalities' in each of the perceptual positions.

SEE	HEAR	FEEL	THINK
Own Eyes	Loud	Emotional	Commenting on them
Like a picture	Sharp	Intensity	Commenting on me
Colour	Dull	Dull	Narrating
Black & White	Quiet	Rough	Questioning
Panoramic	Stereo	Smooth	Lots of Self Talk
Near	Tone	Sad	No Self Talk
Far	Tuneful	Happy	
Large	Harmony	Angry	
Small	Mono	Physiology	
Focused	Pitch	Breathing	
With border	Temp		
No border			
Size			

You may, of course, add more sub-modality descriptions and it make take a few attempts to really get a sense of what changes as you move from position to position.

Exploration

When mediums and psychics talk about what they do they often make a point of saying that they need to be a clean channel. Well could they be talking about the need to be in 'third position' so that they are not responding to their emotions or projecting them onto their clients BUT are remaining neutral to the situation in order to see the situation clearly and so apply intuition and experience to what they perceive?

Now here's the hard bit.

After spending a few days considering these perceptual positions you need to focus your attention on your behaviours.

Take any situation you have been involved where the outcome was not what you had desired; maybe you were not resourceful or were misunderstood.

Consider it carefully.

Now review it from the three different perceptual positions and explore what you said, how you said it, what the other person understood (or not) and how your behaved (your body language, your actions before and after) and your thinking (motivations, agenda).

Of course in second position you will see it from the emotional/behavioural standpoint of the other person and from third position you will see the interaction of the people in the situation.

Not only is a great tool for exploring behaviours and conflicts, but it also allows you to consider how well your behaviour matches your words and hence how congruent you are.

Week Five Focus : Intention

You may have noticed that whereas the first couple of weeks were task-focused, i.e. about doing things; these latter sessions have been about reflection based upon what you have learned and what you are learning.

If we are honest with ourselves every aspect of our behaviour is 'self-serving'. Now I can hear the more literal of you screaming at me 'but I do lots of things for other people without any desire or expectation of reward!"

And of course you do...

But if you stop for a moment and ask yourself "what do I get out of the things I do?" you'd probably be surprised at your own answers.

So of course you engage in 'random acts of kindness', but there is the reward of 'feeling good' about your action; or possibly that you are 'behaving in accord with some personal or spiritual philosophy' – are these not actually serving you and your feelings?

Just because your motivation is hidden within your personality or psyche doesn't mean that it's not there. So whilst you may not consciously process the thought 'If I give blood I'll feel like a better person', it is nevertheless there (possibly).

Some writers will argue that self-sacrifice and altruism is 'hard wired' into the human brain since it has an evolutionary purpose (Dawkins, 1976); which is the survival of the population as a whole rather than the individual within a population... or as Star Trek's Spock might say, 'the needs of the many outweigh the needs of the one'.

If this is true, and I personally suspect it to be so, then it would follow, perhaps, that human-beings also created belief systems which celebrated this unconscious drive and thus necessary behaviours for 'moral', 'selfless', 'sacrifice'.

Far from apparently lessening such acts of altruism, I feel that such insights actually connect us to the natural world and the cosmos rather than setting us aside from it.

OK, so I mentioned Dawkins and it would be beneficial at this point to comment upon his other major work "The God Delusion". In this book (Dawkins, The God Delusion, 2006), he argues that belief in a 'personal God' is a delusion.

He quotes an earlier writer who suggested that 'when one person suffers a delusion it is called insanity, when many people suffer from a delusion it is called religion' (Pirsig, 1991).

Now I feel we must distinguish between religion and spirituality – they are not the same thing.

A religion can be considered as a political organization organized around a value and belief system which has a spiritual core. In many religions the idea of God as a creative, motivating, continual presence and 'parent figure' features with the teachings (or dogma).

For me spirituality is about the idea that there is something 'more' behind the universe (cosmos) which is not understandable to the human mind. This 'something' is more like the way Einstein viewed spirituality – it was not personified in any real sense (as in many religious ideologies), it just 'was' and 'is'.

I assume that Einstein would've been happy with the idea that the more we learn about the nature of the Universe the more we can understand it and the links we have within it.

For me the idea of The Cosmos, The Universal Mind or God, is more about the personal understanding and relationship we can have with it and each other. I am aware that in trying to sense such a relationship I not only anthropomorphize by giving 'it' human (and therefore limiting) qualities but I also 'project' my limited understanding upon it. I may talk about "Mother Nature" or think as many neo-pagans think that there is a creative force behind the universe which we attempt to understand through the personifications we call The God and The Goddess (a natural projection of gender and possibly gender roles which we recognize through the myths and stories we weave).

This is not therefore the God of Religion but a metaphor for something we cannot yet grasp and yet feel connected with.

The occult dictum 'As Above So Below' which has been translated clumsily into practices such as Astrology, simply points out that there is a connection, a cause and effect relationship between life and the universe and not, as so many oversimplifications promote, the idea that 'planetary energies and alignments of planetary bodies' effect the day to day life of the individual.

Astrology is an ego-centric practice developed before it became Astronomy and before Astronomers really tried to understand the workings of the universe. Consider when 'casting' a 'natal chart', the Astrologer will conduct a series of calculations which place the individual at the centre of the solar system. The astrological chart depicts, albeit in a vastly oversimplified way, the dance of the universe around the individual.

For me, it is the mythic, symbolic and metaphorical stories we can create through astrology that are of interest and not the summation (or limitation) of an individual's potential 'through the planetary alignments'.

So, back to the point...

You are obviously reading this book because you have an interest in personal and/or psychic development... but what is underlying this interest?

What is your motivation and intention for developing 'psychic' awareness as defined in this work?

I can tell you my motivations and intentions for writing it and can do so in the following list:-

a) I write to formulate my ideas
b) I like to share my ideas and promoted debate
c) I believe that some words need to be reclaimed
d) I believe 'total sensory perception' enriches **communication**
e) I believe communication is at the heart of **relationships**
f) I believe dogma, **intolerance** and **prejudice** are related
g) I want to combat the 'cult-of-anti-intellectualism'
h) The word **'psychic'** deserves re-definition
i) The word **'spiritual'** has been hi-jacked by fundamentalists
j) The word **'magician'** has been devalued
k) The word **'karma'** has been hijacked
l) A counter to the nonsense of the **New Age Space Cadets**
m) As a counter to the **Cynics and Debunkers**
n) To promote questioning (skepticism)
o) To replace debunking with **skeptical enquiry**
p) To be understood by others
q) To explore what I share in workshops and performances
r) To develop my ideas as a **Rational Mystic**
s) To open a channel for challenge, feedback and discussion
t) To let some ideas out and make room for more
u) To allow others to explore their own communication patterns
v) To allow others to challenge their thinking
w) To add something to the 'spiritual/psychic' debate
x) To challenge an elitist view of 'psychic/spiritual development'
y) To become a better author
z) To earn a couple of pounds (dollars) for my efforts

So there you go 26 motivations/intentions behind the writing of this book. No doubt I could think of more...

So what are your motivations/intentions for engaging in this 7 Step Programme?

Do you want to feel good by helping others?

Do you want to improve your communication skills to understand and be understood by others?

Do you want to become a 'working' psychic and earn some money for your skills?

Do you want to explore your own ideas, values and attitudes?

Do you want to 'learn stuff'?

Do you want to feel enlightened?

AND, here are some big questions...

If you develop your skills as a 'psychic' what difference will it make to you and your life?

If you want to (or currently) works as a 'psychic' what do you want to bring to your clients/friends/customers?

If you start to look carefully at the intentions behind your desires and behaviours I suggest you will begin to have a greater insight into yourself; your relationship with others and the behaviours you engage in.

Now we are back to 'congruence'.

So your task for this week is to consider your behaviours and needs in the light of your personal motivations and intentions.

Are you really getting what you want from your behaviours?

Are you able to consider your own personal agenda when helping others, 'being psychic', 'being spiritual' and engaging in a dialogue?

Are you simply wanting to **promote** an idea, personal belief, agenda or doctrine rather than **simply share** it?

Try to list the things you are 'getting out' of the activities you are engaging in that have a spiritual, magical, psychic focus.

State what your behaviour/action was and then write the reasons, motivations and beliefs behind it (as I did above in terms of writing this book). Aim for 26 items in this list.

Reflect upon what these lists tell you about your 'real' intentions.

Finally consider the possibility of approaching a situation without any conscious or unconscious agenda – how would it be different?

How would YOU be different?

How self-serving are your behaviours even when you make the statement that you have no other intention than 'sharing' the 'love', 'peace', 'calm', 'truth' you have found?

Week Six Focus : Ownership

So we're nearly there...

I wonder if, assuming you have been following this step-by-step process, you have noticed anything different about yourself; your ability to communicate with others and your relationships?

I wonder if you have started to develop what we can call your intuition or you 'psychic sense'?

Are you noticing more in your environment?

Are you listening more?

Are you aware of your personal beliefs, attitudes and agendas and, more importantly, are you able to question and challenge them?

If so you've already started this week's work.

Ownership is really about taking responsibility for your actions, words, thoughts and learning.

To take this idea to another place and time think about this :-

> *"To attain the SANCTUM REGNUM, in other words, the knowledge and power of the Magi, there are four indispensable conditions--an intelligence illuminated by study, an intrepidity which nothing can check, a will which cannot be broken, and a prudence which nothing can corrupt and nothing intoxicate. TO KNOW, TO DARE, TO WILL, TO KEEP SILENCE--such are the four words of the Magus, inscribed upon the four symbolical forms of the sphinx."*
>
> (Levi, 1910)

Ownership or responsibility for one's own actions is one thing, but from a psychic (magical) perspective the four virtues of knowing, daring, willing, keeping silent have a real resonance here.

For me psychic (and personal) development is not about my own personal growth, but since I live within a society, it is also about how I interact (and therefore) effect those around me.

As a teacher I have a commitment to continue to learn for myself and a drive to share ideas with others. Not to persuade them to think as I think, but create questions for them to answer.

In terms of my rational mysticism I accept there are times when I need to pay particular attention to the four virtues as explained by Levi as being the 'Virtues of the Sphinx'.

To Know – is about the continuing quest to discover, learn, develop and experience. It is also to be aware of the impact I have on the world and the world has on me.

To Dare – is about challenging limitations; recognizing the cultural and religious rhetoric which has shaped thinking. It is to risk changing my ideas as I share them and sharing my ideas as I change them.

To Will – is about knowing and understanding you will. This is not simply about the motivations underlying our actions nor the drive we have to met our needs; it is about a sense of purpose behind actions which are not only about material survival. The will is about aspirations, dreams and ambitions which are 'in line' with the ebb and flow of the 'cosmos'.

To Keep Silent – is about being able to keep your truth, your works, to yourself. It's not about not communicating, rather it is about choosing how and when to share. Sometimes the true sage or guru speaks less than the false-prophet. It was Thomas Aquinas who said 'speak your truth gently and if necessary use words'.

Your path of self-discovery, your psychic and personal development, is not necessarily something you get a badge of honour or a scroll of course completion for. It is a never-ending journey for which the rewards are not always those things you can or need to shout about.

Think of your developing awareness as you would a deeply passionate love affair in which everything can be expressed in a touch, a kiss and a moment of tenderness.

So taking by ownership of yourself; your actions, your words, your emotions, your dreams you become more congruent, less needy and more open to the worlds and ideas of others.

You are not angered by the beliefs of others since you are secure in your own.

You are not victim of the projected emotions of others since you own your own feelings.

You are not fearful of your truth since you are open to change, new learning and new ideas.

You are not a fundamentalist or evangelist since you can share your truth quietly and passionately when invited but never dictatorially and dogmatically.

> *"The great secret of magic, the unique and incommunicable Arcana, has for its purpose the placing of supernatural power at the service of the human will in some way.*
>
> *To attain such an achievement it is necessary to KNOW what has to be done, to WILL what is required, to DARE what must be attempted and to KEEP SILENT with discernment."*
>
> (Levi, 1910)

Path Self Discovery : No Badge

Reclaiming The Magician Within

In western culture the archetype of the Magician has been Disney-fied and stripped of all its real power; demoted to a trickster who performs tricks at children's parties.

Magic is Real!

Magic is the art of bringing about change in accordance with will.

In a very real sense we are all magicians since everyday our actions make changes within our world. There is a direct relationship between our intention, our focus, our application and the degree of influence we have on our world.

Understanding the nature of WILL is the journey of the Magician; acquisition of KNOWLEDGE is the desire of the Magician; DARING to challenge and grow is the act of the magician; being quiet in their power is the SILENCE of the Magician.

The Life Cycle of The Magician passes through four stages.

The **Trickster – element AIR**

- Is playful, experimental and quick thinking.
- In terms of 'conjuring' their skill is sleight of hand.
- In terms of esoteric law they are the **Initiate** with Mercurial, airy, qualities.

The **Sorcerer – element FIRE**

- Is dramatic, energetic, sometimes intense.
- In terms of 'conjuring' their skill is illusion
- In terms of esoteric law they are the **Practicus** with Promethean, fire-like characteristics.

The **Oracle** – element WATER

- Is gentle, empathic and reflective.
- In terms of 'conjuring' they are The Mentalist – skilled in the workings of the mind
- In esoteric tradition they are the **Adept** with Odinic qualities of learning and sacrifice

The **Sage** – element EARTH

- Is wise, considered and a teacher.
- In terms of 'conjuring' they are the Master Magician skilled in magic and illusion and knowing the difference between them. They are the philosopher.
- In esoteric tradition they are the **Magus** who engages Socratic questioning and the encouragement of learning through dialogue, trial and performance.

The Magus is aware of the cycles within cycles and so readily becomes the Initiate, Practicus and Adept when new learning opportunities present themselves.

So in terms of owning your own journey, where are you in the different aspects of your life, work and relationships?

Are you able to recognise, encourage and provoke changes within yourself in order to manifest change in the world?

Are you taking responsibility for where you are and creating (considering) actions you can take to move on if that is your will (desire, purpose or self-recognised destiny)?

These are the questions for this week and for you to consider. Remember you can seek inspiration and ideas through 'automatic writing', 'meditation' and 'mindfulness'.

The Elements : Water Earth / Fire Air

This symbol embodies the four elements plus a fifth traditionally considered as aether but now thought to represent spirit

Week Seven Focus : Feedback

So how have you been doing?

This final step is a step which requires you to look again (review) all you have learned.

Ask those closest to you what, if anything, they have noticed that is different about you lately?

Are you finding less conflict, resistance or blocks in your work, relationships and home life?

Are you able to take a 'third position' easily and quickly so that your perception of a person or situation does not become fixed or stuck?

Are you able to create choices in terms of what you say, what you do and what you feel?

Are you being mindful?

Are you being more proactive instead of constantly reactive?

Are you able to listen more than you speak?

And the key question...

Are you becoming aware of others needs, emotions and perhaps 'thoughts'? In many ways this question is to do with your perceptions – and the new ways you may be seeing people, their points of view and their 'agendas'.

7 : Feedback

NOW you can start to put all of these tools into practice and get 'real time feedback' on your increased perception.

When a friend or colleague is talking to you about a problem, take a third position – become clairvoyant.

Develop your clairvoyancy by asking good questions rather than making personally focused judgments.

Ensure that you re-state what you have heard in the words that your friend or colleague used and then summarize the situation so as to ensure you have a better understanding before offering an opinion.

Let me explain what I mean with a simple example...

A friend comes to talk with you about a 'problem' they are having with their teenage son...

Friend :   *I'm really annoyed at Pete right now and things seem to be going from bad to worse; I just can't cope.*

You :   **What is** *Pete doing?*

Friend :   *He's out all hours and just not listening to me*

You :   *And* **is that is what** *is going from bad to worse?*

Friend :   *No, that's just what he's like, but Phil's had his work hours cut so there's less money coming in and managing household bills is getting really tough.*

You :   **So you're** *trying to cope with all of this on your own?*

Friend :   *Yes, it feels like I'm the only one who cares.*

129

You :   **So I hear you saying** – *your teenage son is staying out all hours and not really listening to you and your needs; your husband has had his hours reduced at work so there is not as much money AND you feel like you are the only one who cares about all of this so you're finding it difficult to cope.*

Friend :   Yes that's it exactly...

You :   So **how do you know** *that you are the only one who cares at the moment? Have you spoken to Phil about your feelings?*

Friend :   Well not really...

You :   *I see, and* **what do you think** *is behind some of Pete's behaviour?*

Friend :   Well, he has said he can't stand the atmosphere in the house at the moment.

You :   **What do you think** *he means by that?*

Friend :   Well sometimes there's an uncomfortable silence between Phil and me so I guess it's kind of tense..

You :   **So let me see if I understand** – *Pete is staying out late and not really getting involved in the home because he wants to keep out of the way of the tense atmosphere that exists between you and Phil AND Phil is not earning as much now, money is tight BUT you and Phil haven't really addressed or talked about the emotional or practical effects of this..*

Friend :   Yes I think that's it..

You :   **So what could you do** *to make things easier?* **What would you like** *to be different?*

Ok this is not the best piece of scripting, but it is very similar to a conversation I had been having with someone as I was writing this chapter.

Notice that there is a pattern to the listener's statements and questions. Look carefully at the phrases which have been printed in **bold** type.

Firstly there is no advice being given.

Secondly there are questions about what was said – which means there was less possibility of jumping to conclusions.

Thirdly there was a 'checking for understanding' at two key points.

The comment which started '**So you are saying**' (or **I hear you saying**) was an attempt to offer back what the listener had heard using the same words as the speaker.

This is vital since it allows for the speaker to hear their own words back and it proves that you have been listening and not simply hearing.

The second 'check' is introduced by the phrase '**So let me see if I understand**' in which the situation is restated using the listeners words so the speaker can check for accuracy.

In counseling speak we have paraphrasing and summarizing.

Now if you are being mindful and aware of the communication patters (body language, voice and word use) you can have deeper insights into what lies beneath the words. More importantly this insight fuels your intuition and so opens the way for more empowering questions and a transformational dialogue.

You are demonstrating your presence in the conversation because you are working listening to understand and not to advise.

You are clearly giving attention to the speaker who, in turn, will give attention to your thoughts and ideas.

You are engaging in structured dialogue which requires you to use every facet of your developing 'total sensory perception' in the hope of being able to support another person who is in need of clarity.

You are not taking responsibility for the other person's situation by telling them what they 'should', 'ought' or 'need to do' but you are guiding them to define what it is they need. Which, by the way, helps you decide if and how you can help them.

In essence you are being encouraged to give the same feedback to those you listen to as you have been asked to reflect upon for yourself.

So what about cards, crystals and ...

Many psychics will use 'tools' in which to pique and sharpen their intuition. If they are using these tools effectively then they are not merely props to create an atmosphere of authority, they are additional prompts for questions that could be asked.

Shamanic teachers of all traditions recognise the value of story, the myth and the metaphor of subjective imaginings and use the power from these images to inspire and motivate.

The receiver of the story and the teller of the tale are both active participants in the (therapeutic) drama which unfolds - the "reader" and the "client" in all esoteric readings need to be active re-creators of magic and meaning.

When a reading, which is generally based upon symbolism, is owned by the "reader" it is one dimensional and requires the "client" to accept an interpretation.

However, if that same "reader" explores the symbolism within a clear framework and encourages a shared interpretation of the imagery then both are enriched by the experience - both own the process.

A Transformational Reading is a dialogue and not a simple re-telling of some remembered story or symbolic interpretation. Hence a Tarot 'reader' in such a dialogue will allow the symbols to speak to their unconscious to provoke thoughts and questions which are then shared with the 'client' who is also invited to let the images speak to them.

The resulting discussion, which is facilitated by the 'reader' is dynamic, reflective, challenging and transforming.

(Jones, Transformational Readings, 2012)

So what am I saying?

The tools a psychic may use trigger the unconscious to connect with ideas and images which may be personal or transpersonal in origin.

The processes we have been exploring in this book are ways through which perception of the 'world out there' and the 'magical world of symbolism' in the mind, spirit/heart of the individual can connect to provide new insights and understandings of any aspect of human behaviour, thought and emotion.

If you use tools to support your personal and psychic development then great, just remember that just as words mean what we agree they mean so to do mystical imagery and so called 'tools of divination". AND for me hereby hangs the issue..

Psychic ability (whatever you now perceive that to be) is not about fortune telling but about exploring choices, options and current realities.

Sometimes your personal intuitions about a possible future or probable past are best kept to yourself since they do not help bring clarity to the past, present or future for anyone else.

Remember along with ownership of your skills and talents (whatever they be) comes responsibility.

Remember that your spiritual truth should not get in the way of supporting and helping others who have a different God, different Credo, different Dogma or different perspective on life, the universe and everything.

The key question has to be *'can you help someone without dumping your truth onto them'*.

Intuitions about Past and Future & Silence

Now this is where the 'real work' begins...

In order to be able to develop, improve and increase your psychic ability you need to revisit the exercises described above on a regular basis.

A regular personal *belief and prejudices check* will allow you to keep track of how you have developed in terms of your personal, spiritual and psychic awareness.

Exploring your awareness of and reaction to any particular environment, place or person will sharpen your perceptive skills.

Allow your intuition guide you, but take time to reflect upon the possible source of that information. Try not to limit it to one favoured source (i.e. spirit guide, Ashtar Command, your great great great aunt Martha, your own unconscious... etc) but rather explore the possibilities of different sources of information.

As mentioned elsewhere in this book we are continually receiving information from the outside world (the Cosmos if you like). Some of this information creeps into our conscious awareness but all of it is filtered by our unconscious. That information that which is not presented to our conscious mind resides in the museum of almost conscious experience...

Psychologists describe the idea that information that we have processed but then forgotten about as crypto-amnesia. It's all that stuff that you forgot you were exposed to, but sits within the museum of the mind. When given the trigger this information can simply 'pop' into your head as if from 'nowhere'.

The rationalist in me suspects that a number spontaneous 'knowings' which are often attributed to spirit communication, for example, are really examples of crypto-amnesia at work. However the personal experience of this sudden awareness is what is relevant here and not necessarily the process behind it. (That is unless, of course, you want to use this experience to convince others of your 'special gifts' or as evidence of your own particular belief system).

A Rational Mystic Perspective

Throughout this work I have been taking a rational mystical approach and although I may have shared some of my thoughts on the transpersonal nature of self and the idea of an 'essential you', I do not feel I have been biased to any one specific spiritual belief system.

My thesis is that being psychic is about sensory perception and the way the individual relates to themselves, others and the universe. It's not 'extra sensory' but rather 'total sensory' and as such something we can all develop.

I might suggest that all those who have been open to their total sensory experience are those who we now call psychic, mediums, intuitives, empaths, mystics, seekers.

I might suggest that all those who have, through cultural, social or personal self-limitation, are those who either deny their own potential or seek to limit it in others – through fear, cynicism or denial.

I will suggest that some of the psychic, intuitive, empathic and mystical folk have allowed themselves to be sucked into a one-dimensional idea of spirituality where there is only room for a single truth, a single religion and a single pseudo-spiritual (political) dogma.

For me the wonder and awe is in the beauty of the mind and the incredible functions of the brain. (They are the same).

We are capable of so much creativity, compassion and care...

We are capable of holding ideas and thoughts which are unlimited in their potential...

We have a sensory system which allows us to interact with the world, the cosmos and the life within it and still recognize that our 'understanding' is limited by the limited nature of our perceptions.

And, we are connected to the Cosmos and everything in it – we are part of it.

I believe that no scientist, rationalist or skeptic would disagree with anything I've just said; where the rationalist and the mystic part company is in the understanding or belief in the nature of the Cosmos itself.

I sometimes feel that those 'mystics' who totally ignore some of the science which is generally accepted are perhaps being closed to the real beauty and power of the Universe and The Cosmos,

The 'Past Life' psychic clairvoyant who talks about someone having a previous incarnation as an artesan (or whatever) 2 million years ago (on Earth) is clearly missing out on some science education. We are aware that the oldest remains are no more than 200,000 years old; that the migration out of Africa was about 60,000 years ago and that agriculture (hence settlements) began around 8,000 years ago.

Ok that 'psychic' could say that science doesn't know everything (a really naff argument since science doesn't claim it does) or that 'we just haven't found evidence old enough yet (a possibility of course but one which would require a major rethink of current evidence – and would 'excite' real scientists).

What about the Psychic-Medium who claims life forms which are actually whales and dolphins living on Oceans on Sirius A and Sirius B. Does the 'fact' that these are bodies of hot gas (stars) not have any relevance?

As for all those who talk about the 'advanced civilization' on the Island of Atlantis having crystal power, knowledge of quantum physics and laser (crystal) surgery a million years ago !!! (see above)

Well – there is nothing I can say which will change their belief system and of course they are entitled to it.

But it is a belief system which is not supported by any evidence and a beliefs system which sometimes discourages people from interacting with the world they live on now.

What if, and this sits really well in the light of our discussions, the wonderful ideas of peace, love and enlightenment espoused by the *Atlantean-Sirius Brigade,* are simply metaphors for models of ways of being which are to be seen as inspirations. Hence their visions are not literal but symbolic; not of places within the physical universe but of spaces within the psyche – aspirations rather than lost-pasts?

Is this not an equally powerful set of ideas?

We do need to lament Atlantis since we can choose to create what it (supposedly) represents?

We don't have to seek the truth of past lives but we can be inspired by the stories they tell.

We don't have to believe that angels have wings, but that they represent qualities and aspects of human spiritual potential?

We are in danger, I feel, of projecting so much of our human value system onto a spiritual real, which if it exists, is a distinct and different from us as we are to the ant. We can inhabit some of the same universe but could never fully understand how we perceive and understand it.

As a possibly embittered caveat, most of the psychics, mediums and clairvoyants I know (or have met) who speak of the 'need to free ourselves from the material' have themselves got sufficient material backing (bank accounts, property or wealthy partners) to fly off to Sedona at a whim; take a 'vision quest' in the Amazon to indulge their star-light twinkled world.

They are as far removed from material concerns because of their secure financial position as their spiritual philosophies are from any semblance of rationality.

One of the key spiritual lessons I was offered so many years ago when in Canada and meeting a Shoshone 'Medicine Man' was that spirituality and the connection we can have with the world was pragmatic and simple.

We live on the Earth and so need to respect what it gives us.

We can tell stories of its creation, the wonderful mythic creatures that inhabited it in order to share in the dream and the lessons we can learn from their interactions.

We can choose to perform theatrical rituals or not. A simple word of thanks, a statement of intent or a prayer is a powerful as dressing up and waving wands so long as the focus, will and intent are there.

We can connect to the mystic and mythic world of spirit through creating or entering our own altered states of consciousness. In this world we can be shown many things, reflect upon our path and be guided to understand many things. BUT it is an internal world of metaphor not a literal world of truth.

We can dream dreams which inspire, but to live as if in a dream denies our responsibility to each other and the earth.

When working in my day to day life I can be motivated and inspired by my unconscious and spiritual connections to my stories.

When engaged in spiritual or mystic explorations I can be supported by the material world I co-create.

When I have returned from my reverie I return home and share what I have experienced.

When I return to the stars everything I was or everything I created remains on the Earth and the essential me returns from whence it came.

Seven Principles

The World Is What You Think It Is

There are no limits to creativity and imagination

Energy Flows Where Attention Goes

Now Is The Moment Of Power

To Love Is To Be Happy With Yourself

All Power Comes From Within

Effectiveness Is The Measure Of Truth

Beliefs filter Perception

Perception becomes "Truth"

"Truth" shapes Behaviour

Behaviour defines Relationship

Relationship reinforces Belief

Exercises

This Section of The Book contains a series of exercises and puzzles which will help you explore and develop your sensory acuity; if you like your Psychic Ability.

Try not to take them too seriously and where necessary rely on your intuition rather than your logical mind.

Exercise 1:

Number Telepathy

On the bottom some of the early pages in this book is a random number, the digits have been generated by a random number generator – you may have noticed them as you read the book and wondered what they were all about.

Here's the idea.

Ask a friend to open the book at a random page and to concentrate on the number – this will be the 'target'

Calm your mind and see if you can get a sense of any of the numbers they are thinking about.

This is not easy, but it will give you an idea of what telepathy might be like.

To make it easier for yourself you can ask your friend to focus on one number at a time in the sequence and you call out 1, 2, 3, 4, 5, 6, 7, 8, 9 slowly in time with their breathing.

You may find that something in their body language or expression creates a sense **in you** of the number they are thinking of.

You might like to do the same thing but this time hold your friends hand as you call out the numbers one at a time to see if you can sense differences in the muscle tension.

As an alternative you could ask your friend to write down the random number from the book; hide the paper and then hold their hand as they, taking the digits in one at a time from their number, call out 1, 2, 3, 4, 5, 6, 7, 8. 9 slowly and in sequence.

You might discover that they hesitate or tense just as they announce the number they are thinking of.

Exploration

If you are able to sense, see or know the

number your friend chose at random then brilliant, some form of telepathic connection may exist.

It is more likely however that you found the exercises where you were looking at body language, for example, were more successful. Remember that in the context of this book that is psychic ability – total sensory perception.

What is interesting is that some of you may have found the exercise where you were holding your friends hand or even finger were the most successful.

Well this may be due to the ideomotor response.

We know that when your mind thinks of moving a hand, for example, that signals travel from the brain to the hand in order to prepare it for movement. These 'signals' are so weak that they do not move the hand BUT alter the tension of the muscles in order to be ready to move.

It is these signals that are often seen to be responsible for the movement of a pendulum or even a planchette on a Quija board.

The person is NOT moving their hand consciously, but their unconscious mind is.

Exercise 2

The Pendulum *Knows*

For this you need a pendulum.

Now you may have one already, or you might like to go to the New Age Store and get one.

You could, however use any weight tied to a piece of string or cord.

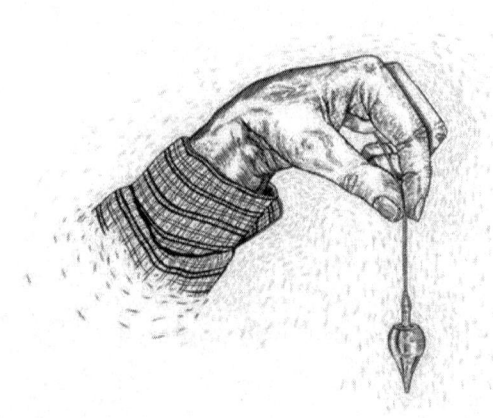

The idea is that you are going to hold the pendulum between your thumb and forefinger and let it swing freely.

Rest your elbow on a firm surface and then simply think about making the pendulum move backwards and forwards. In a few moments you will find that it does so.

Next think about making the pendulum STOP and, as long as you are thinking about making it stop it will.

Now think about making it move in a circle... and yet again it will.

Play with the pendulum until you get a feel for what is happening.

Try using your other hand and see which one is best.

Exploration

This is the ideomotor reflex in action.

In the absence of any other information, it was your mind which caused the pendulum to move. It is important that you are convinced of this before you move on.

Now I can hear 'dowsers' and existing pendulum users saying that the pendulum moves in response to questions asked about specific things so it's not as simple as that. Well maybe, maybe not.

The subject of dowsing is beyond the scope of this book, but since we are talking about communicating with the unconscious mind (and perhaps the transpersonal mind) then the following ideas are valid.

One way of thinking about using a pendulum is to let gain access to your unconscious mind – the information you don't know you know. In some ways this is how a pendulum is used in hypnotherapy.

Exercise 3

The Pendulum *Knows* 2

Sit quietly with your pendulum and then 'ask it' to show you a YES or POSITIVE signal.

Simply think YES and notice which way the pendulum swings. It may be very different for you than for someone else.

Once you are sure you have a YES signal and that it is consistent, do the same with NO.

Simply think NO and notice which way the pendulum swings. Hopefully it will be clearly different from your previous YES signal.

You can also try to do the same for **MAYBE and POSSIBLY** and **DON'T KNOW – CAN'T TELL**.

Exploration

In some ways this further validates the ideomotor aspect of pendulum working, but it also opens out some interesting possibilities.

Since you now have a Yes, No, Maybe and Can't Tell 'signal' you could try asking questions for which you **do not consciously** know the answer.

This is where the 'art of dowsing' can be said to begin.

On the one hand we have, as far as I am concerned, the possibility for the pendulum to answer questions based upon my unconscious (perhaps even transpersonal) awareness to which I am consciously ignorant of.

Using the pendulum this way is fun, interesting and may well lead to some personal insights.

On the other hand dowsers will claim that you can become sensitive to 'earth energies' ; 'spiritual energies' and a whole host of 'energies' we are surrounded by (auras, chakras, personal energy fields and so on).

For me this may (or may not) be the case and since some of these ideas stem from a particular spiritual discipline (or dogma) the discussion is beyond the scope of this little book.

They are interesting possibilities for you to explore however.

Exercise 4

The Emotional Pendulum

Below are a list of emotions, feelings and 'states;

LOVE	DREAMY	ANGER
FEAR	FRUSTRATION	SAD
AMAZED	RELAXED	HAPPY
WORRIED	MOTIVATED	TENSE
CONFIDENT	DISGUSTED	EMBARRASSED
HORRIFIED	HUNGRY	BULLIED
LONELY	HATEFUL	SURPRISED
NEEDY	DESIRED	STRONG
HOPEFUL	INTUITIVE	CLEVER
JOYFUL	SEXY	EXCITED
CONFUSED		

Ask a friend to think of one of these emotions and imagine a situation when they would have felt or would feel it.

Have them hold a pendulum and then show them the words on the following five pages. As them to **THINK YES** if they see the word for the emotion they are thinking of on the page they are looking at.

HUNGRY	SEXY
LONELY	RELAXED
EMBARRASSED	HOPEFUL
DREAMY	WORRIED
SURPRISED	CONFUSED
LOVE	AMAZED
FEARFUL	DESIRED
CONFIDENT	CLEVER

EMBARRASSED	CLEVER
RELAXED	DISGUSTED
NEEDY	DREAMY
CONFUSED	MOTIVATED
LONELY	SAD
INTUITIVE	ANGRY
FEAR	DESIRED
BULLIED	

DISGUSTED	DESIRED
EMBARRASSED	HATEFUL
HAPPY	SAD
TENSE	CONFIDENT
EXCITED	AMAZED
RELAXED	NEEDY
FRUSTRATED	SAD
SURPRISED	CONFUSED

EMBARRASSED	SEXY
EXCITED	DREAMY
DISGUSTED	HAPPY
MOTIVATED	TENSE
CLEVER	AMUSED
INTUITIVE	WORRIED
CONFIDENT	STRONG
CONFUSED	HOPEFUL

HORRIFIED	HAPPY
CLEVER	HATEFUL
HUNGRY	CONFUSED
LONELY	BULLIED
NEEDY	DESIRED
SURPRISED	SEXY
STRONG	INTUITIVE
EXCITED	

Now ask your friend to place the pendulum over each of the words in this list and THINK YES when the pendulum is above the emotional word they are thinking of:-

LOVE	DREAMY	SURPRISED
ANGER	TENSE	NEEDY
FEAR	CONFIDENT	DESIRED
FRUSTRATED	DISGUSTED	STRONG
AMAZED	EMBARRASSED	HOPEFUL
SAD	HORRIFIED	INTUITIVE
RELAXED	HUNGRY	CLEVER
AMUSED	BULLIED	HAPPY
WORRIED	LONELY	SEXY
MOTIVATED	HATEFUL	EXCITED
	CONFUSED	

Exploration

Here's the thinking behind this little experiment.

Firstly you will have information from the pendulum if your friend really thinks of the emotion behind the word they are thinking of.

Now in the five lists the words appear jumbled-up; some are missing and some may be repeated.

As your friend looks at the page you ensure that you gaze at the words (quickly) as well as noticing the YES movement of the pendulum.

You may well form an impression of the word or emotion being thought of. It may help you to ask your friend to 'look' into your eyes after seeing each page upon which the word appears.

Next when you ask your friend to move the pendulum over the final list of words you can watch for any tell tale movements which, when linked with any intuitions you may have already gleaned could give you an insight to the emotion being experienced.

If this does not help, simply ask your friend to give you their hand and read the list of full list of emotional words on page 157 out in any order. As before you may sense 'something' in their being which tips you as to the emotion they are thinking about.

Again remember that we are defining psychic ability here as being a sense, a feeling an intuition which is based upon the sum total of perceptual experience (which includes transpersonal awareness).

Exercise 5 : ESP Symbols

The history of Psi Research contains numerous references to a Dr J B Rhine and Zener Cards.

Originally, tests for ESP were conducted using playing cards. However when this methodology is used, a participant is only credited a correct prediction for guessing both the number and suit of the card. This means that the chance of correctly guessing a card is greatly reduced, and there is a lot of ambiguity involved with statistical analysis.

Another problem with using playing cards was that many people have a preference for a particular card, number or suit and will constantly suggest that as their prediction for the next card that will appear.

This led to the development of a set of cards known as Zener cards, invented by Karl Zener.

A typical ESP/Zener Deck contains 5 sets of cards each bearing a different symbol.

The five different symbols are thus repeated five times in a typical ESP deck.

Whilst the 'favourite card' associations which prove to be problematic in terms of using regular playing cards, it must be noted that some of the shapes within the ESP deck are also being 'prone' to being 'more liked' than others – some are possibly more emotionally appealing than others.

With this in mind, this exercise, is based upon the emotional reaction people have to the shapes.

Ask your friend to look at the symbols on the diagram below and make an emotional choice about which they like best and then draw them on a piece of paper in **their order** of preference.

Then ask them to write an emotional word under each symbol which summaries how they feel about each shape.

Your task is to try to intuit their order of the symbols and the emotional words associated with each.

Exploration

The more you do this the more you will start to recognize common associations and even sequences of shapes.

There is something here about how our unconscious mind processes images and symbols. Indeed there are several 'intuitive and psychic readers' who use ESP cards rather than Tarot or Oracle cards. See (Jones, Transformational Readings, 2012)

In the context of psychic awareness as we have been discussing this exercise will give you deeper insights into the human psyche.

A page on the California State University has this to say on shapes in terms of architecture (CSU, 2010)

Circle
Connection, community, wholeness, endurance, movement, safety and perfection.
Refers to the feminine: warmth, comfort, sensuality, and love.

Rectangle or Square
Order, logic, containment, security.
Rectangles provide a fourth point, which is mathematically the foundation for 3D objects, suggesting mass, volume, and solids.

Triangle
Energy, power, balance, law, science, religion.
Refers to the Masculine: strength, aggression, and dynamic movement

If this interests you then a quick web-search will open some interesting doors for your exploration of shapes.

Exercise 6 : Remote Viewing

Remote viewing (RV) is the ability of seeking impressions about a distant or unseen target using 'psychic-intuitive' means - "sensing with mind".

A remote viewer attempts to give information about an object, event, person or location that is hidden from physical view and possibly at some distance from the 'viewer'.

The term was coined in the 1970s by physicists Russell Targ and Harold Puthoff, who worked at Stanford Research Institute and not as some have claimed Stanford University.

The work at SRI was part of the Stargate Project the umbrella code name of one of several projects established by the U.S. Government to investigate claims of psychic phenomena. The Governments interest was primarily military and of course RV presented the possibility of 'psychic spies'.

The project was closed in 1995 with reviewers stating :-

> *Even though a statistically significant effect has been observed in the laboratory, it remains unclear whether the existence of a paranormal phenomenon, remote viewing, has been demonstrated.* (Michael D. Mumford, 1995)

So here's your opportunity to explore the idea of Remote Viewing.

On the following pages are a series of photographs.

The idea is that a friend looks at one of the photos, concentrating on every detail in the image.

You ask them to imagine being there, being in the photograph and hearing the things they'd hear; feeling the things they might feel and thinking the things they might think.

As they do so, you try to pick on ideas and images that are coming into **your** mind.

Try to keep your questions to a minimum and simply make statements of what you are sensing.

Of course this exercise needs to be thought of as a starting point since there are a limited number of photographs, but you could extend it by collecting other pictures and using them in future 'trials'.

Remember that this is just for fun, so relax and see what happens. It's not a test – simply a game.

HOWEVER, if you think about the things we have been exploring you might like to consider the possible role of non-verbal communication in this exercise. The fact that your friend is being asked to focus on a particular picture and imagine being there will mean that they are creating internal representations of what they are looking at.

In terms of our current definition of psychic ability (i.e. total sensory perception) then this should present no real philosophical challenges.

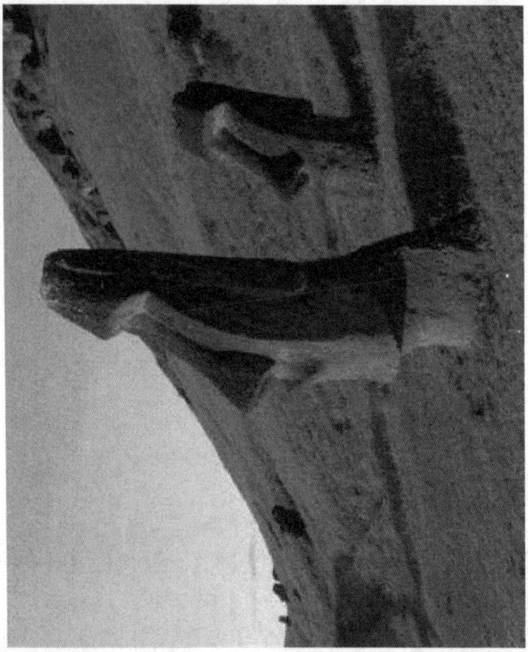

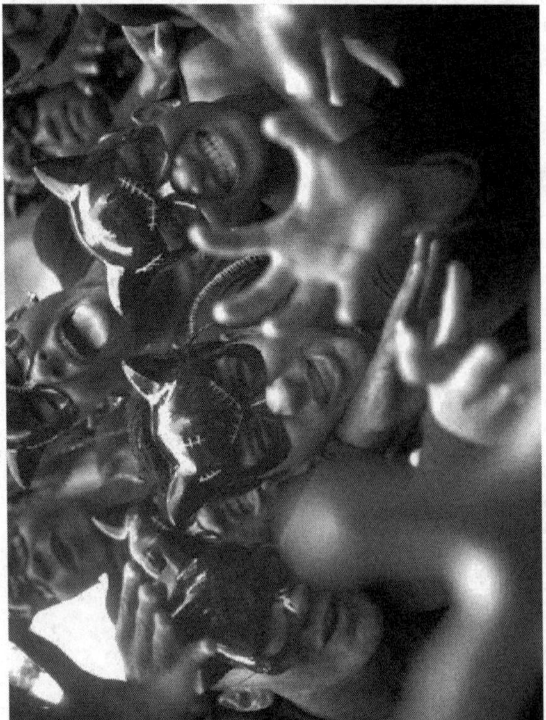

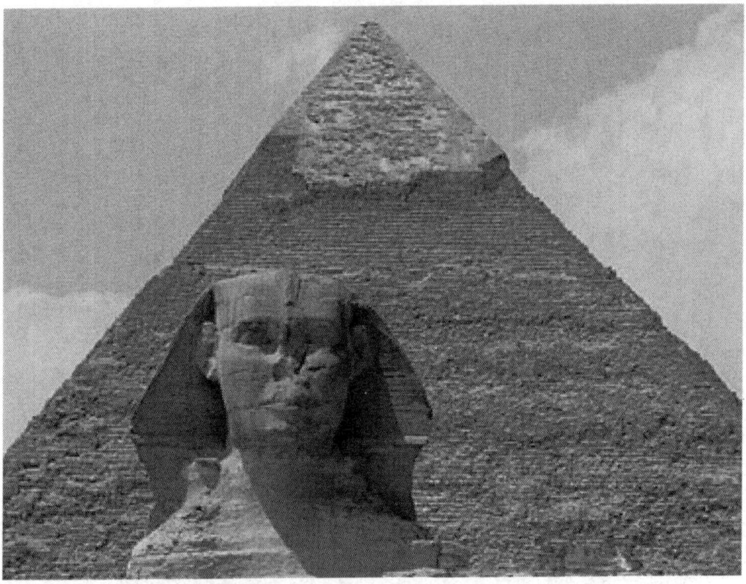

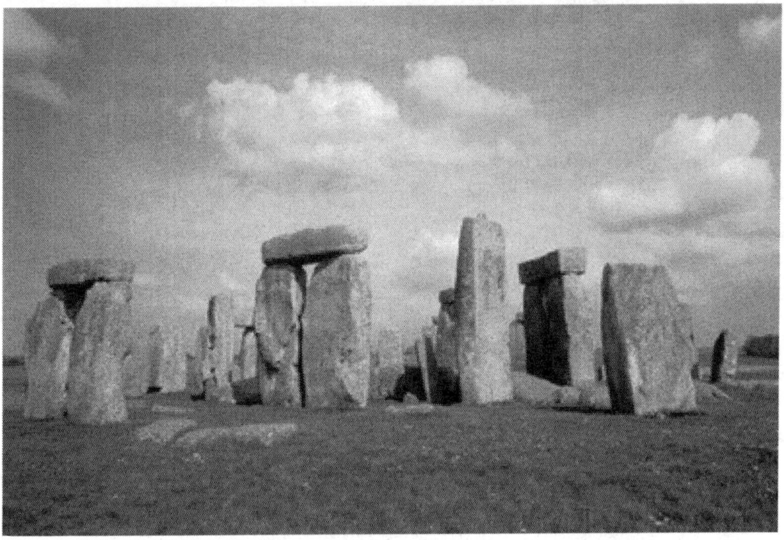

168

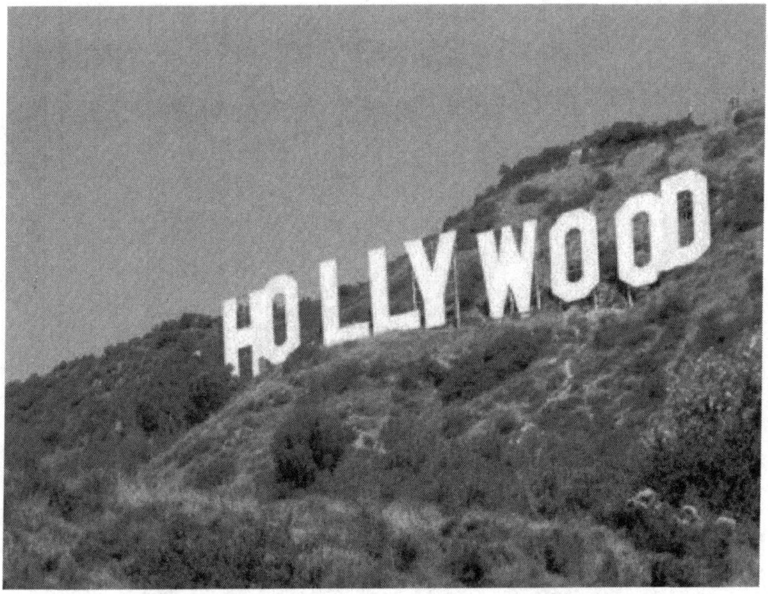
HOLLYWOOD

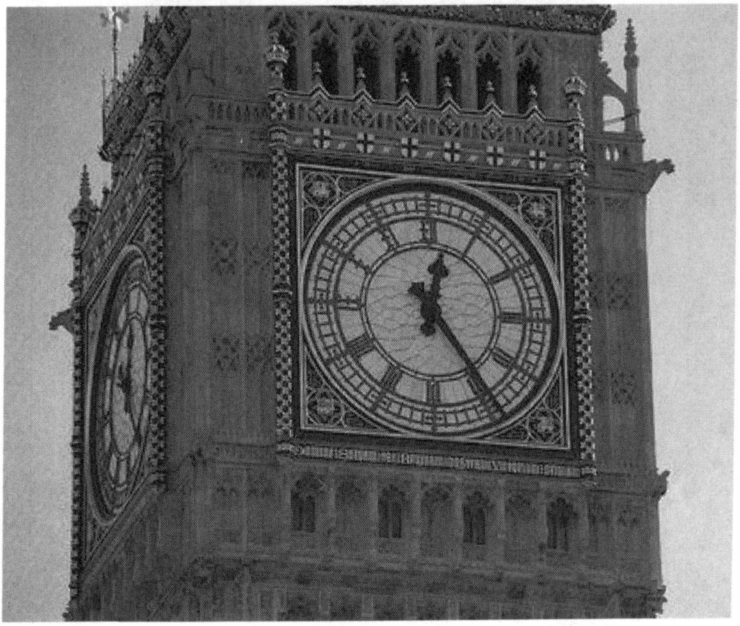

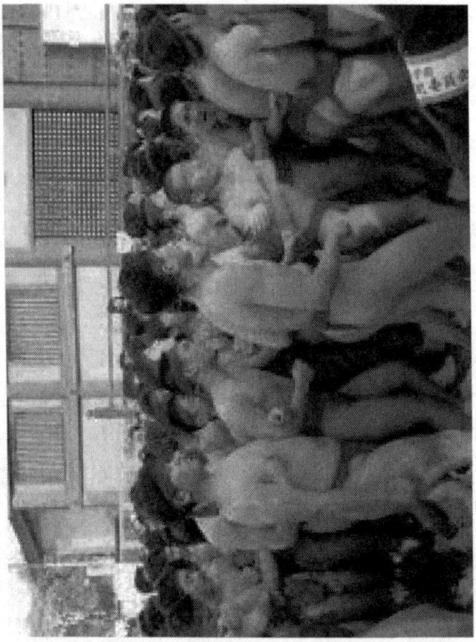

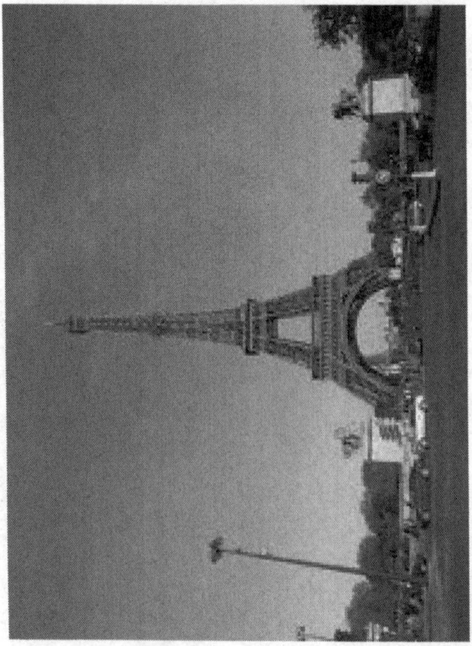

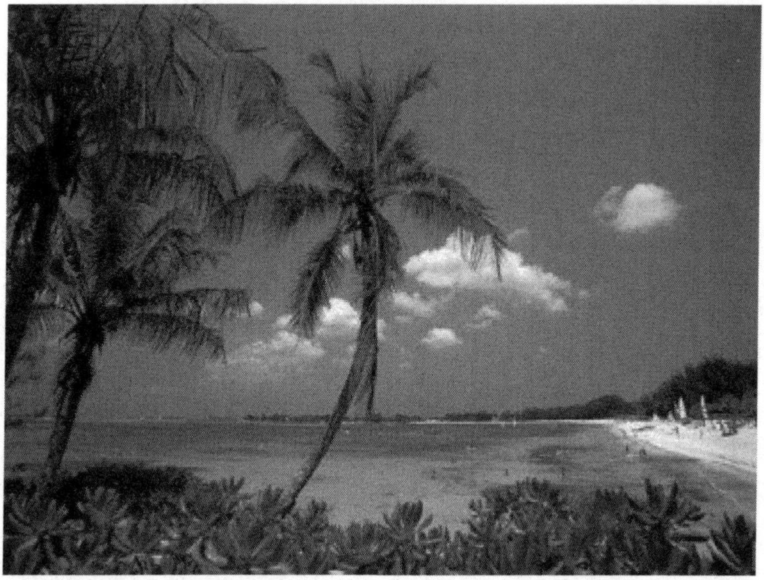

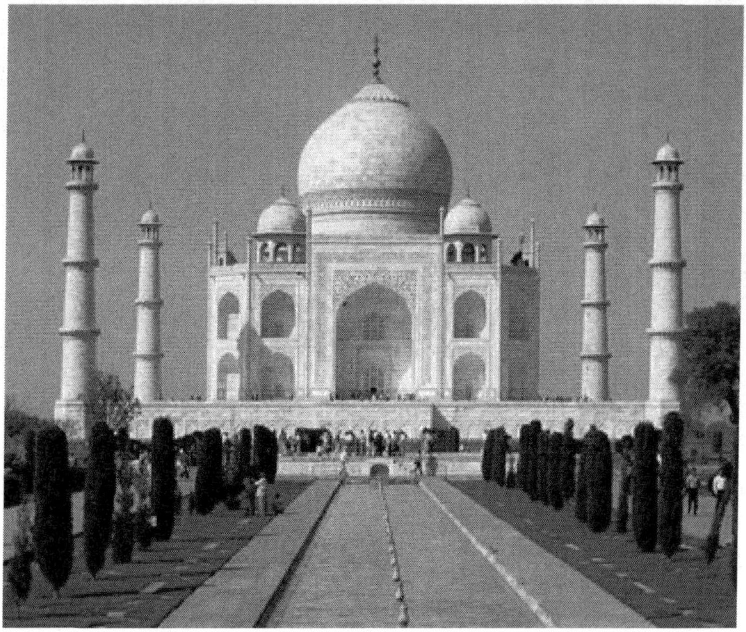

Exploration

In this kind of exercise it would be very difficult to distinguish between information 'assumed' or 'guessed at' because of subtle non-verbal cues and that which is 'known' by other 'intuitive' means.

Since the general thesis of this work is that being 'psychic' is about 'total sensory perception' then all is well. The real issue, I guess, is when you want to defer to some kind of religious or spiritual belief system in order to validate transpersonal/intuitive experiences.

You might find that some people will find it easier to ascribe some kind of emotion to each of the pictures above, so another possibility is to ask the person 'sending' their thoughts to focus on the kind of emotions the picture conjours for them.

If you remember from some of the ideas earlier in this book we spoke of internal experience having 'see', 'hear', 'feel' and 'think' components.

You could ask your 'sender' to imagine themselves there, hearing the sounds and feeling the feelings they would be feeling...

Then ask them to think about what they would be saying to themselves – what would their self-talk be in if they were the person taking the picture?

You may find that you will be able to 'pick-up' on more than just an element of this – you might be able to even speak their thoughts!

Exercise 7 : Being Inspired

This final exercise will hopefully introduce you to the way people can be given inspiration by finding meaning in randomness.

There are many kinds of 'psychic readers' out there some using tools like The Tarot, some using crystals and some using any number of the myriad of oracle cards and stones available.

I was asked recently why do I need to use Tarot cards to give a (transformational) reading to a client. Can't we just talk?

Well of course we can.

But the random (or synchronicity inducing) nature of card selection allows for the unconscious mind to respond to, and find meaning, in a random set of symbols or images. (Jones, Transformational Readings, 2012)

In the same way Bibliomancy, the use of books for readings, has been seen to provide inspiration. In bibliomancy the person seeking inspiration poses a question, which frames the problem, and the opens a book at any page and reads any set of words.

In this way the unconscious mind can be triggered into finding relevance and meaning in the words and phrases which have been generated by a random action.

Psychologically the action of engaging in turning a problem or challenge into a question allows the unconscious mind to consider different perspectives. The randomly produced words (or images created by the words) allows for the minds creative potential to kick-in; for the intuition to be 'turned-on' and any transpersonal (collective unconscious) connections to be made.

Designers and creative people trained in thinking tools would recognize this process as 'forced analogy' a technique designed to kick-start imagination and creativity.

So in this exercise you can ask a friend to frame a question about a personal challenge and/or issue and then turn to one of the twenty or so movie quotes below.

Allow them to read the randomly selected quoted to themselves and see how it fits as an answer to the question.

You could use your developing personal awareness to explore with your friend any creative ideas that come from the selected quote.

Talk about initial reactions, feelings about the quotation itself, and then consider what (if anything) could link to the question which has been posed.

Treat this as a bit of fun and try to avoid the heavy, life changing 'stuff' until you've developed a sense of how this process works.

Once you've used the quotes in this book, you could find another text and see what that gives you.

For Inspiration ....

(1)

KARMA – is not a spiritual bank account into which we deposit our acts of goodness in order to counter past acts of 'non-goodness' but is simply about knowing that this is the place you need to be now. (inspired by The Matrix)

(2)

THE PAST - "Oh yes, the past can hurt. But you can either run from it, or learn from it." (The Lion King)

(3)

TRUST - I'm dishonest, and a dishonest man you can always trust to be dishonest... Honestly, it's the honest ones you want to watch out for, because you can never predict when they're going to do something incredibly...stupid. (Pirates of the Caribbean)

(4)

LOVE – is not an energy or a gift which we can choose to give or receive, but a connection we have with others. The strength and purity of this connection gives love its texture. (inspired by The Matrix)

(5)

BRAVERY - "It takes a great deal of bravery to stand up to your enemies, but a great deal more to stand up to your friends." (Harry Potter)

(6)

REALITY - If real is what you can feel, smell, taste and see, then 'real' is simply electrical signals interpreted by your brain. (The Matrix)

(7)

LEARNING - The greatest thing you'll ever learn is just to love and be loved in return. (Moulin Rouge)

(8)

FINDING LOVE - Love cannot be found where it doesn't exist, nor can it be hidden where it truly does (Kissing A Fool)

(9)

CHOICES - No one can see a choice beyond that which they understand... (The Matrix)

(10)

WAITING - Do you know that place between being asleep and awake, where you still remember your dreams? That's where I'll always love, that's where I'll always wait for you. (Hook)

(11)

PASSION - Love is passion. Obsession. Someone you can't live without. Someone you fall head over heels for. Find someone you can love like crazy, and will love you the same way back. Listen to your heart. No sense in life without this. To make the journey without falling deeply in love, you haven't lived a life at all. You have to try, because if you haven't tried, then you haven't lived (Meet Joe Black)

(12)

SELF-WORTH - Don't let anyone ever make you feel like you don't deserve what you want. (10 Things I Hate About You)

(13)

ENDINGS - "I guess that's what happens at the end, you start thinking about the beginning."

(14)

DEFINING MOMENTS - "When a defining moment comes along, you can do one of two things. Define the moment, or let the moment define you." (Tin Cup)

(15)

CHANGE - You can't change what people are.. without destroying who they were.. (Butterfly Effect)

(16)

LIVING - "The brave do not live forever but the cautious do not live at all." (The Princess Diaries)

(17)

FACING YOURSELF - Calling someone fat doesn't make you any skinnier. Calling someone stupid doesn't make you any smarter. All you can do in life is try and solve the problem in front of you. (Mean Girls)

(18)

BELIEFS - "As we grow older, it becomes difficult to just believe. It's not that we don't want to, but too much has happened that we just can't." (Now and Then)

(19)

SOMEONE SPECIAL - What if someone you never met, someone you never saw, someone you never knew, was the only someone for you? (Sleepless in Seattle)

(20)

WHO WE ARE - It is not our abilities that show what we truly are... it is our choices. (Harry Potter)

(21)

MAGIC - The reason why everyone wants love so much is because it's the closest thing to magic. (Aquamarine)

(22)

REASON - There is no rhyme or reason why something's work and something's don't, why you get something's and why you don't, but life still goes one (Notting Hill)

(24)

SELF WORTH - A gold medal is a wonderful thing. But if you're not enough without it, you'll never be enough with it. (Cool Runnings)

(25)

NO GOING BACK - How do you pick up the threads of an old life? How do you go on? When in your heart, you begin to understand, there is no going back. There are some things that time cannot mend, some hurts that go too deep... that have taken hold... (Return of the King – Lord of the Rings Trilogy)

Exploration

Remember the mind wants to make order out of chaos and is really good at 'pattern-matching' and that is why these apparently random selections of images and words can work well.

Speaking of Synchronicity...

Synchronicity was a concept described by Jung (Jung C. , 1952) in which two or more events that are apparently causally unrelated or unlikely to occur together by chance, are experienced together in a meaningful way.

Jung maintained that just as events may be grouped by cause, they may also be grouped by meaning. A grouping of events by meaning need not have an explanation in terms of cause and effect.

It is the personal meaning and relevance which we can draw from synchronicities that are interesting.

Remember the language of the unconscious mind is the language of metaphor and symbolism, so your psychic development is related to your ability to create meaning from a series of a-causal events. If you allow yourself to get swept away by the apparent cause-and-effect nature of synchronicity you are in danger of falling down a rabbit hole of your own self-reference.

Well that's it for now.

I really hope you have found something interesting, thought provoking and useful in the last hundred or so pages.

Remember the quality of your relationships are directly proportional to your ability to communicate within them...

For me this book has been about communication, improving your sensory acuity and levels of personal reflection. As with so many things within the mystery or esoteric traditions what we have been encouraged to think of as magic is a glittery shadow of what spiritual, magical and mystical development actually is.

We go to the New Age shops and try to purchase instant enlightenment forgetting that it is the personal, psychic and spiritual journey that is important and not the destination.

I'm always happy to hear feedback and welcome your thoughts and comments.

You can contact me via email alan@aljones.net or via social networks such as Twitter and Facebook (alanjonesUK).

My websites are

alanjonespsychic.com and aljones.net

With every best wish

Alan

REFERENCES

CSU. (2010). *Psychological Effects of Shapes*. Retrieved from California State University, Stanislaus: http://www.csustan.edu/oit/WebServices/SupportResources/PsychOfShapes.html

Dawkins, R. (2006). *The God Delusion*. Bantam Books.

Dawkins, R. (1976). *The Selfish Gene*. Oxford University Press.

Durkhiem, E. (1893). *Division of Labour in Society*.

Elert, E. (2013, April 1). *Pop Sci*. Retrieved 2013, from Pop Sci: http://www.popsci.com/science/article/2013-01/emotions-which-there-are-no-english-words-infographic

Gladwell, M. (n.d.). *Malcolm Galdwell Blink*. Retrieved from Malcolm Gladwell: http://www.gladwell.com/blink/

Healey, S. (2005). *Dare to be Intuitive*.

Jaffe, A. (1961). *Memories, Dreams and Reflections*.

Jones, A. (2011). *Ramblings of a Rational Mystic*. Alan Jones ISBN 978-1-300-90507-3.

Jones, A. (2012). *Transformational Readings*.

Jung, C. (1952). *Synchronicity: An Acausal Connecting Principle* . Bollingen Foundation.

Jung, C. (1996). *The Archetypes and the Collective Unconscious*. London.

Lajoie, D. H. (1992). Definitions of transpersonal psychology: The first twenty-three years. *Journal of Transpersonal Psychology Vol 24* .

Levi, E. (1910). *Transcendental Magic*.

Mayho. (1998). *Mayho Clinic*. Retrieved April 17, 2013, from
http://www.mayoclinic.com/health/meditation/HQ01070

Michael D. Mumford, e. a. (1995, September). *An Evaluation of Remote Viewing:*. Retrieved 2013, from Laboratories for Fundamental Research:
http://www.lfr.org/lfr/csl/library/AirReport.pdf

Miller, G. (1956). The Magical Number 7. *Psychological Review 63: 81-97* .

Nathan, R. N. (2008). *Carl G. Jung Man of Science or Modern Shaman*. Retrieved from Crossroads:
http://www.crossroad.to/articles2/08/nathan/jung.htm

Pirsig, R. (1991). *Lila : An Enquiry into Morals*. Bantam Books.

Ramachandran, V. S. (1988). *Phantoms in the Brain*.

Rinpoche, S. M. (2008). *ShambalaSun*. Retrieved December 2012, from How to do Mindfulness Meditation:
http://www.shambhalasun.com/?option=content&task=view&id=2125

Trench. (n.d.). *Trench's New Testament Synonyms*. Retrieved from
http://studybible.info/trench/Natural.